GETTING IN
WITHOUT
FREAKING
OUT

GETTING IN
WITHOUT
FREAKING
OUT

THE
OFFICIAL COLLEGE
ADMISSIONS GUIDE
FOR OVERWHELMED
PARENTS

ARLENE
MATTHEWS

E RIVERS PRESS
ORK

Published in the United States by Three Rivers Press, an imprint of the
Crown Publishing Group, a division of Random House, Inc., New York.
www.crownpublishing.com

Three Rivers Press and the Tugboat design are registered trademarks of
Random House, Inc.

Library of Congress Cataloging-in-Publication Data
Matthews, Arlene Modica.
    Getting in without freaking out : the official college admissions guide for
overwhelmed parents / Arlene Matthews.—1st ed.
    1. College student orientation—United States—Handbooks, manuals,
etc.   2. Education—Parent participation—United States—Handbooks,
manuals, etc.   3. Stress (Psychology)—United States—Handbooks,
manuals, etc.   I. Title.
    LB2343.32M38 2005
    378.1'98—dc22   2005025253

ISBN-13: 978-1-4000-9841-5
ISBN-10: 1-4000-9841-6

Printed in the United States of America

Design by Ruth Lee-Mui
10 9 8 7 6 5 4 3 2 1

First Edition

For Adelaide Moskowitz,
my fourth-grade teacher—wherever she is

ACKNOWLEDGMENTS

I'd like to thank all of the students and families with whom I've worked over the years. We have all learned a lot from one another.

Thanks also to my agent, Judith Hansen of Marly Rusoff & Associates, for seeing the potential in this book; to my editor, Kathryn McHugh, for so diligently and skillfully helping to shape it; and to my copy editor, Carrie Andrews, for making me look smarter than I actually am.

As always, I'd like to thank my family for putting up with maternal absenteeism as I pounded away at my iMac and fielded phone calls from the college-bound and their eager parents.

During all of this, my dog Max served as a peerless under-the-desk foot warmer. My two cats, Ambie and Recess, contributed their usual editorial expertise by walking across my keyboard at every opportunity. Any typos or awkward phrases are their sole responsibility.

Finally—and no kidding—I'd like to thank those exceptional teachers who made a difference in my life as well as those who are now making a difference in my son's life. Thankfully, good teachers are to be found everywhere. Running across one is always a blessing.

[I am] deeply concerned about the level of stress among young people as a serious national health issue.

Robin Mamlet
Dean of Admissions, Stanford

The reason I'm concerned about this is because we're training our children to be the most anxious, stressed-out, sleep-deprived, judged and tested, poorly nourished generation in history.

Marilee Jones
Dean of Admissions, MIT

C O N T E N T S

Chapter 4. **College Matchmaking**

Chapter 5. **Testing, Testing, SAT**

Chapter 6. **Activities Are Supposed to Be Fun**

Chapter 7. **Essays Don't Have to Be Perfect**

Chapter 8. **Procrastination Happens: The Application**

Chapter 9. **Going on Tour**

Chapter 10. **It's an Investment, Right? The Financials**

Chapter 11. **And the Envelope, Please ...**

I N T R O D U C T I O N

How This Book Came to Be—and What It's For

* A seventeen-year-old junior, determined to get a jump on her personal college essay, fears it will be dull because her life lacks personal tragedy. "Why didn't anything bad ever happen to me?" she asks her parents. She adds, with a twinge of hope, "Do you think it still might?"

* A disappointed young woman says the reason she didn't make the Ivies was because she was raised to be a BWRK (admissions-speak for Bright, Well-Rounded Kid). Her mom agrees. "We should have forced you to take viola lessons—or Mandarin Chinese—and not allowed you to do anything else!"

* A senior whose college applications are complete is surprised to receive a congratulatory acceptance letter from a university to which he'd not applied and didn't especially want to attend. His beaming mother explains she'd forged an application on his behalf . . . just in case. A spirited argument follows: Whose life is it, anyway?

* A couple who has already hired me as their son's college coach at the end of his sophomore year calls to apologize: "We gave your name to our friend for coaching, but then we gave her the wrong phone number. We don't want you to work with that family. We think their son and ours might end up applying to some of the same places."

Are these case studies of dysfunctional families? Are they outtakes from a new reality show gone haywire? Unfortunately, no, and no. They're actual—and all too typical—scenes from perfectly normal parents and kids caught in the throes of what might be called college admissions anxiety syndrome.

Several years ago, I took a sabbatical from my Manhattan-based psychotherapy practice to spend more time with my family. For fun, I took a part-time job as an instructor for a national SAT test-prep service (yes, I have a somewhat unusual idea of fun!). On Saturday mornings, I'd attempt to teach the finer points of sentence-completion and reading-comprehension strategies to dozens of high school juniors and seniors who were so worn out from their curricular and extracurricular endeavors, and yet so apprehensive about what lay ahead, that they could hardly decide whether to have a nap or a panic attack.

Subsequently, I created a consulting business called Your College Coach to help college applicants find schools that match their talents and strengths and to assist with the entire applications process. In my new role, I became intensely absorbed in the subculture of college-bound high school students and witnessed firsthand how gearing up for college admissions—and all that the process entails—fills them with dread, desire, doubt, impatience, and apprehension.

Parents of the college-bound, naturally enough, wish they could help. Often they do, although not necessarily in the most productive ways. Accustomed to micromanaging everything from their toddler's playdates to their high school student's choice of AP classes, it's understandable that many moms and dads turn into virtual hovercrafts, looming ominously over their frustrated offspring. But some take far more than a reasonable, supportive role. Okay, I'll be blunt: they're obsessive. When they try to wrest control of the process, family tensions rocket.

Over and over, I've seen admissions mania whip even the calmest, most centered, and down-to-earth teens and parents into an anxious froth. The ensuing family dramas highlight many of the problems underlying the college-application process today: our skewed perspective on what constitutes achievement, our insistence on equating self-worth with a process that is by nature random and chaotic, and a narrow belief in only "good" or "bad" outcomes.

Difficulties and worries are inherent in today's college-admissions process. Unpredictability breeds stress, and in this situation, outcomes are nothing if not unpredictable. This anxiety is magnified by the echo chamber of dire warnings from everyone around, from other parents to college counselors to the media: "Supply and demand factors make getting into college tougher than ever! Freshman slots are in the most rare supply! Your child needs to devote his or her high school career to getting into an elite college—*or else!*"

But is this really the way it is? Far from it. What is true—and what isn't reported—is that there are more opportunities for your child to find a college that matches their needs, aspirations, abilities (and even budget) than ever before. And, as is usually the case, our greatest troubles arise from within ourselves. Approaching the admissions process with a fear-based attitude only compounds the college-bound stress syndrome. When searching for a college, we should view ourselves as discriminating marketplace consumers. Instead, we've resigned ourselves to feeling utterly consumed. There's so much information available, it's tough to sort through it in a meaningful way.

So, here's my position: everybody chill. Is your teen agonizing about fitting in three AP classes next year amid piccolo lessons, varsity basketball, French club vice presidency, hospital volunteering, SAT study, and college-prep counseling? Have you scheduled every vacation from Labor Day to spring break to tour universities? Are you considering taking out a loan just to fund the application fees to your child's "short list" of twenty schools?

A calmer, more balanced approach to admissions can prevail! Indeed, if we allow ourselves to relax about the process, it may offer our kids those valuable life lessons we've been hoping to teach them all along—self-awareness, flexibility, equanimity, confidence, and inner strength.

Why is it so critical to lighten up about college?

* Because anxiety over college admissions is creating rifts in families at a time when parents and kids should be bolstering their relationship in light of the changes ahead.

* Because an exclusive focus on college planning can overshadow important aspects of forging a young person's future identity, in the way that obsessive wedding planning can take the place of psychological preparation for marriage.

* Because emotionally overwrought and physically fatigued high school students are carrying their angst forward into their college freshman year. (UCLA's Higher Education Research Institute and the American Psychological Association say incoming freshmen are reporting more anxiety and depression than ever before.)

* Because the adolescent years are stressful enough without additional self-imposed or parent-imposed pressures about a process over which one has relatively limited control.

* Finally, because worrying obsessively about college won't increase anyone's chances of acceptance, while a sane, measured approach just might.

Getting In Without Freaking Out is your road map back to sanity. It's a companion for all you frazzled parents who long to minimize stress for yourselves and your high school students as together you face the competitive pressures, standardized tests, "senioritis," and the transition from home to campus life. It's part reality check, part consumer education, part emotional comfort food.

My hope is that this collection will help your family regain a sense of control by putting college into a more realistic life context and by taking ownership of the choices you really do have, which are many more than you imagine. You don't have to read the 101 secrets in any particular order, though you can if you like.

The book is meant to be dipped into when you need a moment of grounding, a change of perspective, or a brief foray to the lighter side when you can't bear to open one more brochure.

Chapter 1, "Take a Deep Breath: The Ground Rules for Parents," is an introductory section that includes a general perspective about the whole admissions process that you should keep in mind before jumping in.

Chapter 2, "Look on the Bright Side," is meant to help you further shift your perspective. Come on, things could always be worse.

Chapter 3, "Don't Believe the Hype: The Admissions Game," provides myth-busting facts on rankings, recruiting methods, and the early stages of the admissions process.

Turn to Chapter 4, "College Matchmaking," for de-stressing advice on helping your teen select a good-fit college.

Consult Chapter 5, "Testing, Testing, SAT," for a look at the cult and culture of standardized testing and ways to ease the pain.

Chapter 6, "Activities Are Supposed to Be Fun," tells the truth about the necessity (or lack thereof) of extracurricular activities.

Chapter 7, "Essays Don't Have to Be Perfect," takes some of the mystery out of what to say—and mostly, what not to say.

Chapter 8, "Procrastination Happens: The Application," addresses the intricate agonies of actually filling out the paperwork.

Chapter 9, "Going on Tour," offers advice on campus visits and college interviews.

Chapter 10, "It's an Investment, Right? The Financials," takes a look at the dreaded financials.

Chapter 11, "And the Envelope, Please . . . ," deals with anxieties of rejection, acceptance, and being put on the wait list.

Chapter 12, "There They Go . . . for Now," looks at letting kids go, taking them back, and staying in touch in between.

Finally, Chapter 13, "Extra Credit," sends you on your way with some final thoughts—and a crib sheet.

If this book fulfills its mission, it will help you and your equally overwhelmed offspring survive the high school years feeling more satisfied than stressed, more united as a family, and more positive about the many significant changes ahead. If it doesn't do its job, you can always use it to de-stress in other ways—perhaps fling it against the wall as you endure your frustrations, or bite down on it to keep from grinding your teeth.

But I'm hoping for the former.

Chapter 1: Take a **Deep Breath:**
The **Ground Rules** for **Parents**

Secret #1
Relax: It's Only College

Ever since your child's prekindergarten teacher praised their new-found ability to hold on to a crayon without stuffing it up a nostril, the march toward college seemed an inevitable progression. As high school approached, this progression probably became a preoccupation. You and your offspring have both dreaded and dreamed of this monumental episode. It seems as if everything hinges on what college they'll attend, doesn't it? But calm down: It's only college.

That's right. Only.

Come on, parents, you know the truth, though you've not yet shared it with your sons and daughters. College is the cheese-and-cracker plate of life—a fine, satisfying appetizer, but hardly the most savory or memorable part of the banquet that lies ahead. In terms of sheer proportion, the time one spends at college will comprise four years out of, say, eighty—roughly 5 percent of one's earthly existence (and that's not counting spring breaks, winter breaks, and summers off). This pales beside the amount of time each of your kids will spend pursuing a career or living with their spouse, let alone the time spent sitting in traffic, counting carbo-hydrates, and watching *Friends* in syndication.

I know what you're thinking: No one succeeds without col-lege—and by this you mean financial success. I can't blame you for your pecuniary concerns. College is an expensive investment. It had *better* pay off. No one wants to spend their golden years doling out a weekly allowance to un- or underemployed offspring. But consider the facts: Although college graduates do earn more, studies show that *what* one studies has far more economic impact than *where*. A recent National Bureau of Economic Research study showed that graduates of so-called selective schools boast no earnings edge. And, at last count, the four wealthiest Americans (all self-made) numbered three college dropouts and a graduate of the University of Nebraska.

While there's no denying that going to college is a good thing, it also doesn't hurt to bear in mind that plenty of illustrious people throughout history never even attended college. This list includes Andrew Carnegie, Ben Franklin, John D. Rockefeller, Henry Ford, and Ernest Hemingway (which is too bad, because Ernest would have enjoyed a good keg party). Nine U.S. presi-dents either never attended or never finished college—among them George Washington, Andrew Jackson, Abe Lincoln, An-drew Johnson, and Harry S. Truman.

The long list of ultrasuccessful men and women who never graduated college is rife with innovators, entrepreneurs, and peo-ple who, in general, accomplished what they did by thinking out-side the box. This group includes David Geffen, Ralph Lauren, Steven Spielberg, Woody Allen, Ellen DeGeneres, Tom Hanks, Walter Cronkite, Rush Limbaugh, Steve Martin, Apple Computer founder Steve Jobs, Dell Computer founder Michael Dell, Oracle founder Larry Ellison, MTV founder Bob Pittman, and Debra Fields of Mrs. Fields Cookies. Oh, add Senator John Glenn, who dropped out of Muskingum College in New Concord, Ohio.

Are you still convinced that your child's future success hangs entirely upon receiving a fat envelope from a first-choice school? If so, let me quote H. L. Mencken, who famously contended that the thinking process "has little to do with logic and is not much conditioned by overt facts." But what did he know? He didn't go to college, either.

IT'S WHAT YOU LEARN, NOT WHERE

In 2000, male and female college grads earned 60 percent and 95 percent more, respectively, than high school graduates, according to the U.S. Department of Education. For families headed by two people with bachelor's degrees, the effect on lifetime income is $1,600,000. But, existing research shows that it's not so much which college one attends but what one does with their education.

WHERE CEOS DIDN'T GO

Between World War II and the 1980s, major companies shopped the Ivies for future chief executive officers. Twenty-first-century corporate reality is a different one.

A study by the Wharton School found that in 1980, 14 percent of CEOs of Fortune 100 companies received degrees from an Ivy League school. By 2001, that number was 10 percent. The percentage of CEOs with degrees from public universities soared from 32 percent in 1980 to 48 percent in 2001.

In 2005, Hewlett-Packard filled the job at the top with Mark Hurd, who attended Baylor University on a tennis scholarship. Disney picked a graduate of Denison University in Granville, Ohio. David Edmondson, a grad of Pacific Coast Baptist Bible College of San Dimas, California, took the helm at RadioShack.

Why the trend shift? Those in the know say companies want CEOs who have a good relationship with the rank and file. Some attribute it, in part, to "reverse snobbery" by non-Ivies doing the hiring.

Secret #2
Stress Is a Killjoy

Everyone knows a family that approached their upcoming Disney World vacation with the precision planning of the joint chiefs of staff. Weeks, months, even years before their getaway, they pored over maps and guidebooks, concocting a "maximum rides, minimum lines" strategy.

Their guidebooks advised them to veer toward entrances on the left, because the tendency of most people is to go right. But, when they arrived at the theme park, the family found most of the other visitors had read the same guidebooks. So everyone started going to the left. Except for those who went to the right, because they figured they would outsmart the people who'd read the guidebooks. Except for those who went to the left, because they figured they'd outsmart the people who were trying to outsmart the first bunch. Despite it all, there were lines everywhere *because that's just the way it is at Disney World*—and because, no matter how hard you try, there is simply no controlling the uncontrollable. At the end of the day, however, this family was none the wiser about the ways of the *World*. What's more, they were so cranky and confounded they forgot to have any fun.

Are you sensing an analogy coming up here? Good, because here it is: Successful college planning is like planning a successful theme-park foray. Don't waste time either following the crowd or trying to beat it. Then your experience can be a rewarding one for all.

Look at it this way: Your child is about to go to college, and that's fantastic. They're lucky. Of course success without college is possible, but how nice it is to have the option. The college years can be a fulfilling, memorable time of life. As you know, twenty years from now, they'd do anything to live the experience over again.

You're lucky, too. You have the good fortune to launch your child into the wide world while helping to provide them with a wonderful opportunity to learn, to live among their peers, and to experience for themselves some of that good old college fun that you remember so well.

Some aspects of the college-admissions process are going to be frustrating. The paperwork will be onerous. The odds of getting into certain schools will be humbling. The admissions system will strike you—correctly—as messy and arbitrary. Competitive pressures and a superabundance of advice will be such that at times you won't know whether to go left or go right. These realities are all genuine stressors (i.e., they are factors that *have the potential* to provoke anxiety). Nevertheless, *you have the power to control the level of stress at which you react.* Your kids can tap into that same power, and you can help them to do so.

This sense of self-empowerment, of proactively opting for a sense of calm over a sense of calamity, will be your greatest ally as the college-admissions drama unfolds. With the right attitude, with the ability to hang on to your sense of humor, you and your family will find your way.

It's best to approach college admissions from the start with a mind-set that anticipates challenges and is ready to meet setbacks with resilience. Prepare yourself to be flexible, to improvise as need be, and to stay open to new, exciting possibilities. Sure, you can give in to Disney World–like mania, imagining you can control the uncontrollable. But if that's your approach, know that by the time your kid's freshman orientation rolls around, neither you nor they will have much sense of fun, adventure, or appreciation left. No, make that right. No, left.

WORDS OF WISDOM

Encourage your child to march to their own drummer. Then explain that, no, that's not an extracurricular activity—it's a tried-and-true philosophy.

Secret #3
There's **Involvement**...
and There's **Overinvolvement**

How involved should parents be in their children's college-application process? Some self-reliance purists say you shouldn't be involved at all, that you should let your children do *all* of the work involved in college admissions, from finding appropriate schools to organizing the paperwork to writing every aspect of their applications using all of their own ideas. This, they maintain, begins to build the kind of self-sufficiency that we all want our children to develop during the college years.

I say this is going too far. Sure, you could throw our kids into the admissions fray without offering any guidance and support. You could also have sent them into the seventh-grade science fair with that project they did all by themselves—the one with the known universe depicted in Styrofoam cups and coat-hanger wire. But did you? I'm guessing no.

On the other hand, guidance and support can easily veer off into obsessive control. Sometimes this happens without parents even being aware of it. Here's a handy emotional barometer. You're too involved in your kid's application process when:

* you start to view every natural disaster as a chance for your résumé-building child to start a sock drive.
* you urge your child to write an essay about how awestruck they were during the 1969 moon landing, and then remember, oops, that was you.
* you become so obsessed with taking SAT practice tests that your child has to go out and buy a second copy of the prep book for their own use.
* you keep an extra stash of vocabulary flash cards in your glove compartment/purse/briefcase/bra.
* you spend every night baking pies for teachers who are reputed to write good letters of recommendation.
* you've gotten really, really good at forging your child's signature on applications to schools they're not really sure they want to attend.
* you've quit your job to undertake a summer-long fact-finding tour of college campuses.
* you're firmly convinced your child's college essay should include one or more of the following words: *abstruse, bellicose, effulgent, querulous, ribald.*

Parents can mete out judicious assistance in so many positive ways. You can help your child find schools that are genuinely a good fit. You can offer the occasional reality check ("I love you, but Dartmouth may not feel that way."). You can be the second set of eyes that makes sure reams of paperwork get coordinated, collated, and sent off to the proper destination. You can even get your hands on that personal essay—not as its author but as its editor. (Every writer, no matter how *effulgent*, requires an editor, lest one's prose become *abstruse*.)

If, however, you find yourself becoming overinvolved, seek a diversion immediately. Go to the gym. Walk the dog. Get the car washed. Put in some extra time at the office. Take your spouse out for dinner (but don't talk about your kid). Or read that Russian novel you blew off for Cliffs Notes long ago. I think it starts something like this: "All involved families are alike, all overinvolved families are overinvolved in their own ways."

TAKE A BREAK

Want some theme-related entertainment? Try renting one of these flicks:

The Perfect Score follows a group of kids who hatch a scheme to make off with the answers to an upcoming SAT. In the end, it's a heist movie with a conscience.

Good Will Hunting features Matt Damon as an MIT janitor who turns out to be a mathematical genius. Robin Williams plays a huggie-bear therapist who helps the savant sort out his life.

The Freshman follows a naïve first-year student from Vermont who gets mugged on his first day at a New York City college. He needs money in the worst way, and he gets mixed up with organized crime.

With Honors teaches some life lessons with panache. The premise: A Harvard student crashes his computer and then loses his only hard copy of his thesis. Joe Pesci plays a homeless man who gives it back to him a page at a time, in exchange for shelter and food.

Breaking Away is the truly heartwarming tale of four nineteen-year-olds who don't know what to do with themselves after high school. Although they live in a college town, higher education is not for them—until, in the end, it is for one. You'll learn a little something about class snobbery, and a lot about bicycle racing.

Back to School stars Rodney Dangerfield as a business mogul who never got his college degree. He pursues it late in life as the result of a challenge from his son. This is a really goofy one—and may be just what you need.

Secret #4

It's Not **Where** You Go, It's **Who** You Are

Okay, you're a grown-up. You've been living and working in the real world for quite some time. You often meet people in business and personal situations. You meet them on planes. You meet them at the gym. You meet them at meetings. When was the last time anyone began a conversation by asking you where you went to college? If you're like most busy, accomplished adults, this topic probably hasn't come up for years, decades even.

Now think about the people you spend time with—your neighbors, your workout or golf buddies, fellow parents from the PTA and school sports events. Think about the people you work with, and even the people you work *for*. Did you ever ask them where they went to college? If you did, do you remember their answer now, or has it gone the way of so much other superfluous information (i.e., has it fallen into an abyss between two brain cells, never to be retrieved)?

The reality is that in real life there comes a point where college credentials cease to matter much. What you've done speaks for itself. Where you began to learn to do it (if indeed that was college at all) is irrelevant.

What your friends want to know is are you good company, are you a good sport, will you help them out when they need to move a large piece of furniture? In the workplace, what people want to know is have you delivered and will you continue to? The bottom line doesn't care if your pedigree is state college, community college, Ivy League, or the college of hard knocks.

I can, however, probably predict the *next* time you will have to say where you went to college. You'll have to divulge that information on your kid's admissions applications—mostly because schools want to know if they are looking at a legacy applicant. After that, no one will ask you about it for a long time, perhaps ever. Remind your high schooler of that once in a while, and remind yourself as well. Today's "most important thing ever" issue can be tomorrow's forgotten factoid. Often it helps to take the long view.

WORDS OF WISDOM

It's not as easy for your child to take a long-term perspective as it is for you. That's simply because they haven't been around as long. So, try playing this little game with them: Ask them to name three people they admire and have them tell you why they admire them. Then ask them where those people went to college. Odds are they won't have the vaguest clue.

Secret #5

You Know You'll Still **Love** Them,

Wherever They Go

Are you one of those parents who has sometimes fantasized about your kid getting into a school so impressive you'd hand out logo-emblazoned ball caps and bumper stickers to every one of your relatives (PRINCETON GRANDMA!)? When you started putting money into their college fund, did you secretly wonder if your investments would cover the course of—say it—Harvard? Have you had recurring nightmares about attracting stares of blatant pity at your local supermarket should your child attend a safety school? That's okay. You're not alone.

But also know you're not alone in this: You'll love your kids exactly the same whether they spend their undergraduate years in the Ivy League or at East-of-Nowhere U. Make sure they know that, too. College-bound kids are putting enough pressure on themselves without worrying that lack of admission to their (or your) first-choice school will render you the laughingstock of the local Stop & Shop.

As a parent, I'll hazard a guess as to what's making you so jittery—and potentially so annoying to your high schooler—right about now. In large part, it's anxiety about how much you'll miss your kids when they're gone. Obsessing on their college applications, essays, and standardized tests is in many ways easier for us than processing the fact that soon our children will no longer inhabit their rooms on a full-time basis. (Never mind that we've been dying to get in there for years, if only to fumigate and to find out whatever really happened to that pet hamster, Zoe.)

Also, somewhere along the line, our culture became so irrationally competitive about parenting that some of us think where our kids attend college is indicative of whether or not we did a good job of raising them. It's a tough racket, parenting. There's always an expert around to claim that whatever we did led our kids toward attention deficits, lactose intolerance, poor taste in nose rings, and a future driving tractor trailers. If you're wondering whether or not you did a decent job of raising your children, ask the real experts: them. (They'll probably say something like, "Heck, yes, until you started leaving those flagged copies of *Study SATs in Your Sleep* on my pillow.")

Consider this: Studies show a healthy relationship between high school kids and their parents is a *far better predictor* of academic success than standardized test scores. It's fine, commendable even, to support your kids in the college-admissions process, but if you feel compelled to get them in a choke hold while you extol the merits of yet another "reach" school, you may seriously want to consider curbing your enthusiasm.

Here's a good rule of thumb: Give your kids a break and let them give you one. Take an occasional respite from application trepidation, and instead make some good memories they can take with them wherever they go. Besides, if you're really nice, maybe they'll finally tell you the whole truth about the hamster incident.

IT'S OKAY TO LET GO A LITTLE

A study reported in the *Journal of Educational Psychology* examined connections between college students' adjustment, success, and their relationships with their parents. It found that students' high grades, confidence, persistence, task involvement, and rapport with their teachers were generally predicted by the extent to which their parents granted them autonomy, while being both demanding and supportive.

The study's findings suggest that a middle-of-the road parenting style plays a role in students' academic success.

Secret #6

Anxiety **Loves** Company

More and more companies—law firms, banks, investment houses, and other big businesses—are offering college counseling as an employee perk. No, it's not for employees who want to return to school. It's for employees with kids approaching high school graduation. The companies contract with college-counseling organizations that offer on-site seminars in subjects like application preparation and financing a college education. Many also offer Web-based workshops and one-on-one counseling, either on-site or via phone or e-mail.

Why are employers doing this? Bottom line: They know that if you're an employee with a college-bound kid, you're going to spend a whole lot of time (yes, some of it company time) researching schools, downloading applications, proofreading essay drafts, and just plain obsessing. By formalizing and facilitating the process, they gain back more of your time and more of your productivity.

They're just being practical. You should be, too. If your employer offers this service, take full advantage of it. If they don't, and your company is large enough to support it, request it. It will give you a lot of information in a structured amount of time, help you get a grasp on what's ahead of you, and possibly keep you from heading down some blind alleys. Even more significantly, it will acquaint you with colleagues who are in the same boat as you. Now when you pass each other in the halls, you can give the high sign and perhaps take a moment to commiserate. Maybe you can sneak off to the copier room and do some deep-breathing exercises.

Of course, many people work for companies that are too small to spend money on this kind of service. Contracts with college-coaching companies can range anywhere from $15,000 to $500,000, depending on the exact services and the number of employees involved. But if you're entrenched, or about to be so, in your kid's admissions process, you should still think about reaching out to associates to see who might be willing to share information—or at least share your pain.

Group support can be incredibly reassuring—ask anyone who's ever been to Weight Watchers. Hunger loves company. So does admissions anxiety. Sharing war stories with colleagues will probably afford you lots of occasions to blow off steam, to conduct reality checks, to feel understood, to find out that other people's kids are as difficult to deal with as your own, and—with any luck—to have a few good belly laughs over lunch.

Secret #7

Freak-Out Moments Are Okay

Despite this book's best efforts, sometimes your kid—perhaps even you—will just want to scream. So here's permission to go right ahead. I mean, try not to do it at the mall or the movies or anything, but having an occasional catharsis in the privacy of your own home won't hurt.

Ahhhhhhhhhhhhhhhhhhhhhhh!

It may even make you feel better.

PRIMAL SCREAM HAPPENS AT COLLEGE, TOO

At midnight on the Sunday night of finals week at Columbia University in New York City, students routinely let out earsplitting screams that echo through the school's normally tranquil Morningside Heights neighborhood. "It's not really clear when the tradition started, but Columbia students have been screaming for decades," a longtime Morningside Heights resident explained to National Public Radio.

"Screaming is always good, especially during finals, like a bonding activity," said a Columbia senior.

Chapter 2: **Look** on the **Bright Side**

Secret #8

College Planning Means More Family
Togetherness

Think the American family is disintegrating? In a study of the national work force, the Families and Work Institute found that children are receiving one hour more of parental attention on workdays than they were twenty-five years ago. Working mothers spend 3.4 hours a day with their kids, and working dads now spend 2.7 hours. Those statistics, of course, are an average. When kids are applying to college, you get to spend much *more* time with them.

How will you spend it? You can apply pressure, invoke guilt, argue, and nag. You could say things like:

* "I saved my whole life so you could go to college, and you don't even appreciate it, do you?"
* "If I'd had your opportunities, there would have been no stopping me."
* "All I want is for you to be happy—so why are you looking at me like that?"

But why go for the obvious? Be a contrarian. Vow up front to add some quality to the quantity of family togetherness during this process.

In the best possible scenario, parents can help kids imagine a future filled with challenge and promise, with increasing self-reliance, and with opportunities to meet amazing new people and do incredible new things. Poring over college catalogues together can be great fun and might even call up a few of your favorite anecdotes about when you were in college (well, not *that* one, or *that* one, but I'm sure you'll think of something).

Don't forget to break for snacks and a little trash TV. Who knows? If you get them loosened up enough on tortilla chips and amateur talent competitions, they may even give you a rare glimpse of what's actually going on inside their heads. (I know, it's frightening—but fascinating, too.)

It may be a long while before you ever have this kind of time together again. Don't squander the opportunity by recriminating your kid or yourself. Try not to set up high-stakes scenarios that ensure disappointment. Don't waste this time being fearful, as that never helps anything. Above all, cherish the spontaneous moments that seem gloriously unproductive, for they can turn out to be the most productive of all.

COLLEGE MEDIA TRAINING ACTIVITIES

What to do during hangout time? You can prep your kids for college life, and experience it vicariously yourself, by tuning in to coed tube fare. According to Student Monitor, the TV shows most watched by college students as of 2004 were *American Idol*, *Friends*, *The Simpsons*, *The Real World*, *The Osbournes*, *The Sopranos*, *Saturday Night Live*, *MTV Cribs*, and *Road Rules*.

If you're more of a reader, the top two college magazines are *Cosmopolitan* and *Maxim*. The top newspaper is the *New York Times*—but 52 percent of college students say they don't read a newspaper at all.

Secret #9

You Can Let Go of "I Didn't Homeschool" Guilt

More than 1 million students are being schooled at home, says the U.S. Department of Education. And guess what? Admissions officers at some very selective schools are liking them. In 2004, Stanford University accepted 26 percent of the thirty-five homeschoolers who applied—nearly double its overall acceptance rate. Harvard's been on board for quite some time and has accepted at least ten homeschooled students in its freshman class as far back as 1996.

What's *not* to like? Homeschoolers are routinely scoring higher than the national average on SATs and the ACT, and admissions officers have publicly praised their preparedness, motivation, and intellectual independence.

But, wait: you didn't homeschool your kid, did you?

I know, I know. You had your reasons, as I had mine. We had busy and productive lives of our own. We didn't want to overtax parent-child relationships that were already so complex. We didn't know what we would do when the math curriculum got as far as pre-algebra. Finally, we didn't know if our systems could handle all the anti-anxiety medication that spending an extra six hours a day with our offspring would require.

Well, it's too late now. But look on the bright side: Before applying to colleges, many homeschoolers are enrolling at courses in local universities to show they can handle the academic and the social aspects of on-site schooling. You already know your child understands the ins and outs of school schooling. Had you kept them intellectually independent at home, they may never have learned:

* how to space out in class but not look sleepy enough to get called on;
* how to bang on a locker so it opens without the combination;
* how to send text messages and listen to iPods without being detected;
* how to get the other kid in trouble for something they did themselves;
* how to schmooze lunchroom ladies into giving them a bigger helping of Tater Tots;
* how to convince a phys ed teacher that they didn't forget their gym clothes, these *are* their gym clothes.

So, stop feeling guilty. Your school-schooled kids will go off into the world armed with a wealth of street smarts that they could have gained only outside the range of your doting parental eye. You've got to believe these smarts will come in handy at some point—especially the Tater Tots thing. Plus *you* never had to revisit quadratic equations or dissect a frog on the kitchen counter. I'd say it's been win-win. But if you don't agree, there's always, you know, home college.

HOMESCHOOLERS HAVE ADMISSION STRESS, TOO

The number of students participating in homeschool education rose from 850,000 in 1999 to over 1.1 million by 2004. College applications from homeschooled students continue to increase. By 2004, 97 percent of colleges reported receiving as many or more applications from homeschooled students as they did in 2003.

Due to the steady increase in homeschooled-student applications, between 80 and 90 percent of colleges have formalized admissions standards for this demographic group. Homeschooled students must submit standardized test scores and a formal transcript of grades to substantiate their academic achievement.

Secret #10

Obstacles Have **Merit**

In his book *The Heart of the World*, explorer Ian Baker recounts his journey in search of a remote, unmapped Tibetan land. Ancient texts repute the destination to be a kind of earthly paradise. There were many obstacles in the path of Baker and his traveling party, the members of which included a revered Tibetan lama. One obstacle in particular made a unique impression. Baker cites a companion's journal entry:

> Sloshing along the muddy trail in the pounding rain, I came upon a large, slimy log that had fallen chest high across our brush-choked path. I viewed the log as a menacing obstacle that was clearly separate, in my way and against me. With no way under or around I jumped, stomach first, and slid over the top.

Regaining his balance, the writer confesses to being enraged at the mud that covered his body. He cursed the log that had so worsened his predicament.

Then along came the lama, Kawa Tulku. As the muddy scribe watched, hidden from view, Tulku tried, and failed, to jump the log from a running start—ending up on his back in a large puddle and laughing uproariously: "Staggering to his feet . . . [the lama] repeated the same maneuver—with the same results—no less than three times. With each collapse back into the puddle his laughter grew stronger and louder."

On the fourth attempt, the lama succeeded, though he landed headlong into another puddle on the log's opposite side. After wiping himself off and before proceeding on his way, he turned, paused, and "lovingly patted the log like it was an old friend."

Getting into college is also a frustrating, muddy process. It involves a challenging journey toward a longed-for destination. Obstacles will inevitably impede any would-be student's way. But how one deals with those obstacles is a choice. They can be resented or embraced. If the latter approach is taken, the student's goal is, in a way, already attained.

If you let it be, any obstacle is itself an education—an opportunity to share a laugh.

WORDS OF WISDOM

. . . frame your mind to mirth and merriment, which bars a thousand harms and lengthens life.
—William Shakespeare, *The Taming of the Shrew*

A merry heart doeth good like a medicine.
—Proverbs 17:22

Numerous studies suggest that situational laughter is an effective coping mechanism for temporary stress. In addition to helping us confront life's challenges, laughter truly does have a salutary effect on health. It boosts antibody levels and immune system functions, and it's a mild form of aerobic exercise.

Secret #11

The System Could Actually Be Worse

In the *New York Times* "Ethicist" column, October 4, 2004, a reader asks:

> A friend from Nigeria wants to go to college to study medicine and has asked me to help him. Unfortunately, Nigerian universities are notoriously corrupt. Many young people are forced to bribe professors and university officials to gain admittance. Wouldn't I be contributing to a corrupt system by helping my friend bribe his way into the university?

With regard to the above ethical quandary, *Times* columnist Randy Cohen advised that the writer help her friend, adding quite sensibly, "It is unreasonable to demand moral purity from the victims of a corrupt system or to insist that they defer college until utopia arrives."

So, you see, it could be worse. In America it's a certainty that faculty members are not on the take. If they were, they might wear clothing that bordered on the fashionable or drive vehicles that didn't merit frantic weekly calls to *Car Talk* that inevitably begin with "I have a 1991 Volvo wagon with a hundred ninety thousand miles on it . . ."

Thankfully, the guardians of America's academe are notoriously fashion-phobic and automobile oblivious. It's not that some of them wouldn't enjoy a good flip through *Vogue* or *GQ* but, hey, there's already a fresh *New York Review of Books* by the bedside. And what's the point of coveting an Audi A8 when you're busy constructing a superconductor particle collider in the garage?

Bribery? I don't think so. Good thing, because you know what happens once you start down that road. No matter how much any of us might be able to ante up—albeit under outraged protest—there'd always be some other parent with deeper pockets or a bigger home equity line of credit.

Every once in a while, when you glean a glimpse of what constitutes reality elsewhere, you remember to be at least fleetingly grateful for the system we've got, warts and all. As for that Nigerian kid, I think he should consider coming to school here. Hours of standardized testing, an agonizing essay, and a plethora of paperwork won't seem like a day at the beach, even to him, but it would beat the alternative. And us? We'll get future doctors, statesmen, scientists, scholars, and leaders who got into school the old-fashioned, if newfangled, way—without shelling out payola.

FYI

The American Association of University Professors titled its *Annual Report on the Economic Status of the Profession, 2003–04,* "Don't Blame Faculty for High Tuition." While tuition and fees rose by about 14 percent at public universities and colleges and 6 percent at private institutions in the 2003–04 year, the Association reported that professors' salaries increased only 2.1 percent (0.2 percent above the rate of inflation). The average salary for a full professor with a doctorate was $88,591.

Secret #12

The SAT Could Actually Be Worse

The first president of the Educational Testing Service, Henry Chauncey, actually had a bigger—much bigger—idea. He wanted, as Nicolas Lemann writes in *The Big Test*, "to mount a vast scientific project that [would] categorize, route and sort the entire population." This was to have been accomplished by administering to all Americans a series of multiple-choice tests, the "census of abilities." The resulting scores would suggest what role each individual should play in society. The eventual legacy of this idea is the SAT.

What is your reaction to this?

A. Get real.
B. And I thought our SAT was bad!
C. All multiple-choice tests are predicated on a fallacy—they are more about time-management skills and short-term memory than intelligence per se.
D. Is one of these the right answer? Because I'm getting nervous.

Secret #13

At Least They Played Musical Chairs

You remember it; your college-bound kid is old enough to re-member it, too: musical chairs. Yes, musical chairs—an amusing and harmless (or so we thought) diversion for young children, who enjoyed (or so it seemed) the thrill of giddily propelling themselves toward a diminishing row of seats in hopes that they would land their little behinds in one and play another round of the game.

Now musical chairs has fallen from favor. Well-meaning pre-school and kindergarten educators have exposed musical chairs for what it is: a cruel, emotionally abusive, and politically incor-rect torment masquerading as a party game. It *excludes* people. It's *random.* It's *unfair.* It's, it's . . . too much like real life and will therefore make children cry.

The thing is, though, have you ever actually seen children cry when the music stops and they fail to plop their *glutei maximi* down in the nick of time? I never have. I've seen them groan, scream, stomp their feet, and stand aside to watch the rest of the merriment—all the while bearing up like little soldiers and, in fact, having a grand old time. They get it: Not every kid's a winner every time in every circumstance, and it's okay. It's so-called grown-ups, projecting their own emotional preoccupations onto kids, who don't get it. Left to their own devices, kids are more sanguine and resilient than most adults can even begin to imagine.

Happily, our sons and daughters spent their formative years in an era where early childhood educators had not yet perfected the art of sheltering them from any semblance of reality, nor devoted so much time to sparing what are thought to be their unfathomably fragile feelings. If our kids' nursery school was the school of hard knocks, they're that much better prepared.

Because now they're in the real world of college admissions. There are more kids circling each row of chairs than there are chairs to be had. Some will plop their rear ends down exactly where they want them to be; others will have to seek another seating arrangement. Not everyone will win every time, under every circumstance, and—even though it may make their parents want to cry—it's okay.

Moms, dads: Let the music begin.

CHILDREN TRAUMATIZED BY POULTRY

Along with musical chairs, the ax has fallen on duck, duck, goose. According to the National Association for Sport and Physical Education spokesperson Paula K. Kun, "[These games] don't belong in a quality physical education program because they eliminate kids."

Flash Card

It's All About Vocabulary—the "A" Words

Acquiescence—The attitude most parents want from their college-bound adolescent.

Assiduousness—Likewise.

Admonishment—What you may be tempted to give a kid who's not displaying acquiescence or assiduousness.

Analogies—Something you no longer need to know for the SATs, so forget about them.

Anachronism—The act of continuing to study analogies for the SATs.

Antediluvian—A period so long ago there were no SATs.

Articulate—What you hope your kid will be during admissions interviews.

Abstemious—What you hope your kid will be at frat parties.

Agitated—The way you will periodically feel as your kid applies to colleges.

Ad nauseam—Latin phrase describing something that goes on to an extreme or annoying extent.

Abdicate—Something parents are not allowed to do, even on days when they are agitated ad nauseam.

Ambivalent—The way you'll feel on the day it really dawns on you that your kid is going away to college.

Acanthopterygians—Fish with spiny-rayed fins and toothed scales, such as mackerel, perch, or bass. (Go ahead, impress your friends.)

Chapter 3

Don't Believe the Hype:

The Admissions Game

Secret #14

College Rankings **Don't Lie,**

They **Mislead**

Every year, high school students and their parents wait anxiously for publications that rank America's "best colleges." Okay, we all like lists: Sexiest People, Worst Dressed, Top 100 One-Hit Wonders. But college rankings tell you far less than you imagine about *what you need to know*. Take them with a huge grain of salt (one of America's top ten condiments, I ought to mention).

One element that factors heavily in a school's ranking is the achievement level of the students it accepts, based on class standing and standardized test scores. Another is the school's acceptance rate, or selectivity—the total number of students admitted divided by the total number of applicants. So, let's think about it: The high rankings that result from attracting high achievers compel more high achievers to apply. Now the school has an even larger pool from which to choose, and so its selectivity will, ipso facto, rise. All of this results in capturing an even higher slot in the rankings, placing the college-ranking game on the list of Most Blatantly Self-Fulfilling Prophecies of Our Time.

What else do the rankings really rank? Things like alumni giving, expenditures per student, and percentage of faculty with a terminal degree (which, I know, sounds like a deadly fever but actually signifies a consummate diploma such as a Ph.D. or an M.B.A.). In short, rankings measure what goes *in*, but not what comes *out*, of a school. This is tantamount to recommending a restaurant based on the ingredients stocked in its kitchen without ever sampling the fare.

How effectively do a school's students use available resources? Do they have access to faculty members outside of class? Do they *enjoy* their classes? Do they take advantage of enrichment: pursue internships, study abroad, participate in research? Are they applying the knowledge they've acquired? Are they pleased with their college experience overall, or would they rather have spent four years apprenticing with a Nepalese cave yogi? These are the questions, my friends. These, in fact, rank high on the list of Most Meaningful Questions to Ask About a College.

Take a few long deep breaths before you peruse those "best colleges" lists. Letting them skew the course of your kid's life would be about as wise as agreeing to let your offspring have extreme plastic surgery after they've watched *Top Celebrity Medical Makeovers*. Lists are fun; lists are interesting; lists can be a useful starting point for your own research. And that's the complete list of What Lists Ought to Do for You.

WORDS OF WISDOM

I am extremely skeptical that the quality of a university—any more than the quality of a magazine—can be measured statistically.
—Gerhard Casper, former president of Stanford University, in an open letter to *U.S. News & World Report*

POPULARITY OF NATIONAL NEWSWEEKLIES:
A RANKING

1. *Time*
2. *Newsweek*
3. *U.S. News & World Report*

Secret #15

Not All Invitations Are Inviting

Greetings! I'd like to invite you to a party at my house.

Well, no, not really. I'd like to invite you to apply *to come to a party at my house.*

Actually, my house is kind of small, so I can only accommodate a few party guests. In truth, I get to be extremely picky about who they will be, since my parties are quite popular. But, I've heard nice things about you, and, hey, who's to say you haven't got a shot?

Do you have any special qualifications that would make you an ideal party guest? I'd love to hear about them. If you like, I'll send you an application to fill out. Oh, and there's a $75 application fee.

But, as I say, my parties are highly rated. You're probably excited that I even sent you this invitation to apply for an invitation. Tell the truth: You are, aren't you?

Every year, high school students who've scored well on PSATs, SATs, and ACTs receive letters from institutions of higher learning that invite them to apply for admission. You might think such missives would come mostly from schools that actually needed more candidates to apply. But no. Some of the nation's most selective colleges do the most postal prospecting.

In 2004, MIT sent a hundred thousand such letters, although its entire undergraduate population consists of just over four thousand students. Harvard sent out seventy thousand. As usual, Harvard got about twenty thousand applications and rejected some 90 percent of them.

Why are schools that are notoriously hard to get into trolling for more applicants? Rachel Toor, a former admissions officer at Duke, wrote in her book *Admissions Confidential* that "the reason [Duke does] recruiting is to get the BWRKs (bright, well-rounded kids) to apply so we can deny them and bolster our selectivity rating." *Ouch*. And then there's math. Any high-scoring SAT-taker can—and should—compute the product of twenty thousand applications multiplied by $75. *Double ouch*.

It's hard for a kid, especially one who has worked hard and actually does deserve kudos, not to feel flattered by these carefully worded ("Congratulations on your academic achievements") love notes. Heck, I get a little puffed up when a new food and wine magazine tells me it is reaching out to discriminating diners. But I usually manage to restrain myself from sending back the reply card.

If your kid gets letters from highly selective schools that don't really seem within the realm of possibility, you're allowed to feel somewhat pleased in spite of yourself. So is your kid. Go ahead, enjoy the moment. But then get a grip. Imagine the equally intense emotional impact of a rejection letter down the road. And teach your child one of the primary lessons of consumer protection: Beware the flattery of perfect strangers.

MORE MATH

Each year, some sixteen hundred colleges buy student names and addresses from the College Board. The names are sorted by subcategories, such as zip code and ethnic group. Sixty-four million names per year are sold at 26 cents per name, for a total revenue of more than $16 million.

According to the National Association for College Admission Counseling, 70 percent of private schools spend $1,000 or more on recruiting for each entering freshman.

Secret #16

A Caltech Reality Check

A few years back, a change in the scoring formula for per-student expenditures caused Caltech to surge from ninth to first place in *U.S. News & World Report*'s list of best national universities. Suddenly, certain parents with little interest in this school before became obsessed with their children applying there.

As of the 2005 list, Caltech had slipped back to an eighth-place ranking. But since you never know what rankings-formula change awaits, the following public service guidelines have been prepared to help you determine whether or not your child should consider applying to the California Institute of Technology:

Kids Should Apply If:	Kids Should *Not* Apply If:
They are seriously inclined toward quantum physics.	They kind of liked *Star Wars,* especially R2-D2.
They would enjoy taking a seminar taught by a Nobel laureate.	They have nothing against Nobel laureates, unless the class is early in the morning or, you know, hard.
They always won first prize at the high school science fair.	They would have won a prize if the dog did not eat their project—and die.
Their social life revolves around homework.	Their social life revolves around their fake ID.
They do not mind the lack of fraternities and sororities.	See above.
SURFing means Summer Undergraduate Research Fellowships.	Dude: *No, it doesn't.*
They appreciate the fact that Caltech was where Einstein adopted the expanding universe model.	They worry that the expanding universe model means Miss Universe is putting on weight.
They appreciate pranks like the Caltech annual pumpkin drop, in which a pumpkin is immersed in liquid nitrogen for days and then breaks into shards when it's dropped from the roof.	Now we're talkin'!

FYI

The California Institute of Technology has an undergraduate population of a thousand. It is one-quarter the size of the Massachusetts Institute of Technology (MIT). As of 2004, it accepted only about 450 freshmen—brilliant techies, all.

Secret #17

They Don't Have to Reach for the **Stars**

Standard advice to every college aspirant is to apply to at least one "reach school." In a perfect world, this might be interpreted as including among one's target schools one that, while by no means a sure bet, is at least within the realm of the possible.

In itself, that isn't a bad idea. After all, one never knows if a particular aspect of an application will hold special appeal—for example, playing an instrument that is badly needed in the school orchestra (glockenspiel, anyone?). But even if such a beneficent coincidence should occur, keep in mind that the student's high school grades, AP test scores, and standardized test results would need to be close to those of the school's general student population. Most schools are unlikely to admit a student whose stats indicate that they simply will not be able to keep up with academic requirements, glockenspiel or no. It wouldn't be fair to the student.

Nowadays, in the grips of admissions mania and trophy-school lust, many parents pressure their kids to take the "reach school" advice to extremes. If you're going to reach, they think, reach really high. So, students with perfectly respectable but unexceptional academic records often take a "what the heck" shot at schools that are so selective they routinely reject valedictorians.

What are we reaching for? The problem, of course, is that many students don't even *want* to go to these schools but feel pressure to at least apply, anyway. It's a waste of time, a waste of paper, and a waste of a $75 application fee. Of course, everyone is welcome to expend their resources as they choose, but also consider that it can often be a sure setup for disappointment. Is it worth the money and the stress to say, "I was rejected by Princeton?" Instead, why not spend the money and expend the effort in adding one more realistic good-match school to the list?

EXCEEDING YOUR GRASP?

Before encouraging your son or daughter to apply to a certain reach school, have them ask themselves these questions:

1. Do I really have a conceivable shot?
2. Is there anything in my application to compensate for less-impressive academic accomplishments?
3. Would I be totally demoralized by a rejection?
4. Do I actually want to go there if I get in?

Secret #18
Some **Bloom** Later

When do most people do their most outstanding work? When are they most creative? It seems as if colleges looking for exceptional freshmen expect the answer to be "already." In reality, research shows that people diverge widely on when they begin to engage in their most successful and creative endeavors. Some begin early and peak early; others start later and peak later. Dean Keith Simonton, a professor of psychology at the University of California at Davis who studies age and achievement, says, "Some late bloomers will not get into full stride until they attain ages at which others are leaving the race."

Need some examples of late bloomers? Cervantes completed *Don Quixote* at age sixty-eight; Verdi wrote *Falstaff* in his eightieth year; Humboldt finished his final volume of *Cosmos* when he was eighty-nine. Grandma Moses started painting in her late seventies. Some people, like George Washington Carver, work in their fields for years only to gain recognition later on. Others, like

McDonald's founder Ray Kroc, find their biggest success following a change of career path.

Studies have revealed that even as some young people shine in specific areas of skill, older folk are more likely to possess wisdom, erudition, and the ability to express themselves fully. They're also better at social skills and diplomacy and in situations that require mining a vast store of knowledge.

So, if your child does not appear to have found their niche by age eighteen, I wouldn't worry about it. In fact, I'd be rather pleased. Peaking at eighteen can make the balance of one's life seem like a fairly boring prospect. It's nice to have something to look forward to.

Secret #19

Every Good College Is Full of Rejects

By now you've surely heard a lot about the college supply-and-demand issue. The number of high school graduates is on the rise because the population of eighteen-year-olds is on the rise. Over the first decade of this century, we're looking at a projected 9 percent increase in high school graduates, and lots of them want to go to college. To complicate matters, more of them than ever are vying to get into so-called elite schools. This makes it harder for any given applicant—your kid, for example—to penetrate the traditional upper strata. All true.

On the other hand, the top tier of colleges is expanding. We want our kids to go to prestigious schools, and so many of them shall—because more and more schools are gaining prestige. All those leftover smart kids have to go somewhere, and as they do, *they* elevate the status of their schools.

A decade ago, for example, no one would have given credence to the idea of "public Ivies." Now, if you tell your friends and neighbors that your son or daughter is bound for the University of North Carolina at Chapel Hill or the University of California at Berkeley, you practically get a genuflection in response. The University of Virginia, the University of Michigan, the University of Texas at Austin, the University of Wisconsin at Madison, and Penn State merit serious claps on the back. Even much-maligned New Jersey (I'm allowed to say this because I live there) earns a solemn nod of respect both with Rutgers University and with the increasingly competitive College of New Jersey (formerly Trenton State).

It all makes sense. Schools at every level are being blessed with "rejects" from the level above. Those kids bring to whatever school they attend not only their intelligence, but also a powerful motivation to expose the folly of the people who didn't accept them elsewhere. It's the American way. Can't get into the country club? Let's start our own country club. Can't get cast in the big show? Heck, let's put on a show right here in the barn!

And what about the kids who used to be able to get into second-tier schools and are now edged out? Happily, the same dynamic holds true. The schools at which they enroll will be given a boost by an influx of bright, determined upstarts. And so it goes down the line.

More kids going to college? More schools raising their standards? Is that a bad thing? Sure, to a parent hovering over a kid who is hovering over a pile of applications. It seems scary at first, but when you think about it, the silver lining shines through. As a society, we can't help but benefit from more schools catering to more and more motivated youngsters. I say hooray for all those "rejects." They will widen the playing field. They will inspire excellence wherever they go. They will put on a show in the barn, all right, and I for one bet it gets a standing ovation.

FYI

Put in historical perspective, the current number of high school graduates is only reflective of an increase in U.S. population, not of a significant increase in the percentage of students who graduate each year. The number of students who graduated from high school in 2003 (2.986 million) is nearly equal to the number who graduated in 1972 (3.002 million). The number of high school graduates actually peaked in 1977 at 3.15 million.

What is different today is the percentage of high school graduates moving on to college immediately following high school. This number has increased steadily since 1976.

Secret #20

Accept That the Process Is Flawed

In Buddhism there is a saying: Every situation has eighty-four problems. The first eighty-three are specific to whatever the situation is. There are multiple difficulties associated with any endeavor. (If you don't believe me, try installing a new printer cartridge, switching your long-distance provider, or having your car inspected.) As we say in America, "It's always something."

The eighty-fourth problem, however, is the same in every situation. The eighty-fourth problem is *We don't want to have any problems.*

Of all the frustrations and difficulties your family will encounter as your child applies to college, the eighty-fourth one is the one most under your control. Accept that there will be problems. Railing against the inevitable amount of random unfairness to which your child will be subjected will only make you crazy. On the other hand, once you accept that things are as they are, you're immediately down to only eighty-three problems.

Every little bit helps.

Secret #21

Harvard's for **Slackers**

What do you say to an obnoxious parent whose kid got into Harvard and who drops it into the conversation every thirty seconds?

Congratulations on your kid getting into the fourth most selective school in the country.

Yes, fourth.

Philadelphia's Curtis Institute of Music and the U.S. Coast Guard Academy take only 7 percent of applicants. New York's Juilliard School takes 9 percent. Harvard accepts between 10 and 11 percent of applicants.

Ha!

A LIST FULL OF SURPRISES

As of 2004, these schools were cited as having the lowest acceptance rates in America, thus being the toughest to get into:

1. The Curtis Institute of Music (Philadelphia, PA) accepts 7 percent of applicants, all extraordinarily gifted musicians.
2. U.S. Coast Guard Academy (New London, CT) accepts 7 percent based on merit. There are no congressional appointments.
3. The Juilliard School (New York, NY) admits 9 percent—all aspiring performers. Auditions and personal interviews required.
4. Harvard University (Cambridge, MA): About twenty thousand apply annually, but only 11 percent get in.
5. Princeton University (Princeton, NJ) accepts 12 percent of the fifteen thousand or so who typically apply.
6. Columbia University (New York, NY) admits 12 percent of applicants—the vast majority from the top 10 percent of their graduating class.
7. Stanford University (Stanford, CA) accepts 13 percent of about nineteen thousand applicants.
8. United States Naval Academy (Annapolis, MD) admits 13 percent of applicants, all of whom must obtain a nomination from a congressman, senator, or the vice president of the United States.
9. Cooper Union (New York, NY) accepts 13 percent of applicants and provides tuition-free education in art, architecture, and engineering.
10. Yale University (New Haven, CT) admits 16 percent of some thirteen thousand applicants.

Secret #22

Chances Are, They'll Get In

The College Board confirms that applications will continue to rise faster than openings at most colleges through at least 2010 and that most schools are more selective than they were ten years ago. But 80 percent of additional applications in recent years have gone to 20 percent of schools. It's the so-called highly selective schools where applications have skyrocketed, for example:

* In 2003, Williams College received 5,341 applications for 533 freshman slots.
* Boston College got 22,400 applications for 2,250 freshman openings.
* Georgetown received more than 15,000 applications in 2002 for a freshman class of 1,485.

In other words, a minority of students trying to get into a minority of schools is fueling admissions hysteria across the country. As the number of students applying to selective schools swells, those schools ipso facto become more selective. The result is like tulipmania in seventeenth-century Holland. During that period in history, members of Holland's upper classes developed a liking for the fragile blossoms and began importing them at extravagant prices. Soon people of all classes began converting their property and cash into flowers. Needless to say, this did not end well.

People overvalue what cannot be easily obtained, sometimes to the point of hysteria. But there are twenty-three hundred four-year colleges in America, and eighteen hundred two-year colleges. With a little care and a little calm, everyone will find a school that suits them. Pick flowers and schools with prudence.

GOOD ODDS

Despite these daunting numbers, the mean selectivity rate for colleges nationwide is 69.9 percent according to the National Association for College Admission Counseling. Two out of every three applicants *are* accepted!

Flash Card

It's All About Vocabulary—the "P" Words

Pretentious—Wearing a "Harvard Mom" cap, even if you are one.

Pejorative—Snide remarks made about the college your neighbor's kid is going to.

Pedagogues—Detail-oriented educators who you hope will write your kid glowing letters of recommendation.

Precocious—A quality always attributed to children by their grandparents, but not always, alas, by their pedagogues.

Pithy—Something your kid's essay ought to be.

Prosaic—Something your kid's essay will be if you insist that they write about their devotion to community service.

Perfunctory—The kind of glance an essay will get if it's prosaic.

Perdition—What you fear will happen if your child fails to do well on the SATs.

Petulant—The way you feel when you see a thin envelope from your kid's reach school.

Psychotropic—Drugs capable of affecting the mind.

Philosophical—The only approach to the admissions process that will keep you off psychotropics.

Chapter 4: College **Matchmaking**

It's **Good** to Get Engaged . . .

Q. What's more relevant to your kid's choice of a good-fit college than newsweekly "best college" rankings?
A. The National Survey of Student Engagement.

Known as the NSSE (sounds like "Nessie"), this survey, funded by the Pew National Trust, polls real live freshmen and seniors at various schools. It poses questions on topics like how students really spend their time, what they like and dislike about academic and nonacademic life on campus, how students, faculty, and staff relate; and how much learning goes on outside the classroom.

NSSE has collected in the neighborhood of three hundred thousand surveys from over six hundred four-year colleges since the year 2000. But don't get too excited—yet. Many leading schools have declined to participate, and some participants opt not to share the results (as NSSE's rules allow). Hmmmm. If your child is interested in a school that won't engage with NSSE or that won't talk and tell, you might want to ask, Why the heck not?

The more parents ask for NSSE results, the more administrators will have to pay attention. Don't be shy. Would you want to buy a product from a company that would not share results of a customer-satisfaction survey? Or that wouldn't even conduct a customer-satisfaction survey in the first place? I'm thinking no.

Ironically, parents compound the college-bound stress syndrome by viewing themselves and their kids as passive supplicants in the college-selection process, letting the colleges do all the selecting when they're about to hand over huge sums of money—not to mention an impressionable human mind—to these institutions for four years. In a twist on consumer culture, people who spend enormous energy comparison shopping for minivans, computers, and cell-phone plans that are customized for their families abandon such practical strategies when it comes to college shopping.

You like to shop, don't you? Some of us were born to do it. Well, think of this as a really big shopping excursion. Find out if schools have features that suit your child's intellectual, social, physical, and emotional requirements. Find out if their customers would recommend them. And let the schools know that the more they help you in such endeavors, the better you're apt to feel about them.

Remember, your kid is about to embark on a long-term relationship with a college. Don't let them jump into this marriage without first getting engaged.

GET DEEP

For information on colleges with the best practices for undergraduate learning, see the report from the Documenting Effective Educational Practices (DEEP) project. DEEP is an in-depth study of successful educational practices at twenty different colleges and universities, all of which had higher-than-predicted graduation rates and high NSSE engagement scores.

There's a comprehensive look at the study in the book *Student Success in College* by George Kuh, Jillian Kinzie, and John Schuh. The book can be ordered via the NSSE website: http://www.indiana.edu/~nsse.

Secret #24

. . . But a Wedding Is **Not** a Marriage

Imagine giving your kids this advice: "When you get married, focus on the really important thing—a big, showy reception. Never mind long-term compatibility. It's the public kickoff that counts. Spend all your time and effort worrying about what you'll wear, what the color scheme will be, what will be on the menu, and what the invitations will look like. Then you'll be happy."

Sound a tad superficial? Uneasy about letting your kid tie the knot with just about anyone agreeable to a Venetian dessert buffet and red cummerbunds for the ushers? Then don't let them, or yourself, be tempted to approach college planning the same way.

Today, obsessive focus on wedding planning too often takes the place of emotional preparation for marriage. Once the chocolate ganache has been polished off and the last stretch limo has departed, brides and grooms find themselves somewhat daunted—perhaps aghast—at facing the reality of constructing an entire life with their wedding partner.

Likewise, our culture's obsessive focus on getting into college—especially a school whose reputed merit will elicit kudos from friends and family—can deep-six important emotional preparation for the years that lie ahead. In those years, kids who have always had beneficent moms and dads hovering about will also have to construct new lives for themselves. As they forge their personal identities, you will have to deal with their startlingly palpable absence from your household.

It's easy—tempting, in fact—to delay thinking about any of this by devoting 99.9 percent of every family member's brain cells to *getting in.* But think, too, about getting through. Devoting some of your conjoint energies and engaging in a few meaningful discussions of the looming college years—complete with all their pending rewards, challenges, and adjustments—can provide all of you with a certain amount of psychological shockproofing and will lead to wiser choices about the long-term compatibility of students and schools.

In the long run, a wedding reception is, literally, a piece of cake. A marriage is more complex. But when the right match is made, it's safe to hope the best is yet to come.

Secret #25
Trophy Schools Are Like Trophy Wives

How is a trophy school like a trophy wife?

* One looks good on your résumé, the other looks good on your arm.
* They both turn your peers green with envy.
* They're both very seductive.
* They're both very expensive.
* They both may put more energy into recruiting new prospects than they put into you.

Secret #26

Don't Follow the Crowd

Aside from "It's highly ranked," there are other dumb reasons to apply to a school. Among them:

1. It has a really good basketball/football/fill-in-the-sport team.
2. They have really good concerts there.
3. Such-and-such celebrity went there.
4. It's a great party school.
5. Lots of my friends are applying there.

The first four seem self-explanatory *(don't they?)*. The fifth may seem to appear a justifiable rationale but is the most self-defeating reason of all.

Sure, there might be some positives about heading off to college with a pack of one's closest pals. Ready-made camaraderie would provide emotional continuity, a jump start on freshman social life, and a buffer against the onslaught of the new and unfamiliar. It would probably make you feel better, too, if your child went off with a buddy, the way they did on field trips and camp adventures.

On the other hand, college offers a wonderful opportunity to forge one's personal identity anew. Heading off to school with companions from the past can make one reluctant to try out new roles and get involved in new activities. This can be especially true if friends from home become roommates. Both may get stuck in a rut (or one may change drastically, generating a schism). People tend to stick with what's comfortable if they can; when necessity forces them to improvise, they blossom.

Then there's this reality: Many colleges limit the number of applicants they will take from any one high school or geographic area. Applying to a school because "everyone else is doing it" may make your child—and you—feel temporarily secure. But why court demographic disappointment? Besides, if your child is passed up for a friend, or vice versa, the friendship may be compromised, at least temporarily. Is it worth the risk?

If a popular school is absolutely right for your child, an application is, without a doubt, worth filing. But if applying there is based on a wish to be one of the crowd, steer them from the lemming-like approach. And don't worry: They'll find friends wherever they go. You did.

HOW ONE COLD SCHOOL GOT HOT

In 2004, officials at SUNY–Buffalo allowed MTV to film a reality show on campus during rush at two of the school's Greek houses. *Sorority Life* and *Fraternity Life* turned out to be a public-relations bonanza. High school kids from all over the country besieged admissions officers, and traffic to the prospective-students page of the university's website tripled. A larger-than-expected percentage of kids who had been accepted decided to attend, boosting the school's yield.

Suddenly, the University of Buffalo, an urban campus located in a part of western New York that, for much of the year, is frigid was hot.

Secret #27

Ask What Your College Can Do for **You**

Selective schools that already have far too many applicants do a disproportionate share of direct marketing and public relations, but some marketing is actually conducted by schools that need more students. Yes, there *are* such schools. Many exist in places like Nebraska, where the state's population of eighteen-year-olds is on the decline.

Sadly, some of the applicant trolling done by schools in such situations has been in notably questionable taste. At Doane College, about twenty-five miles southwest of Lincoln, Nebraska, school officials apologized after receiving complaints about recruiting postcards featuring a student football player surrounded by attractive women and encouraging students to "play the field." The cards were sent to about 13,500 prospective students in California, where the number of high school graduates is on the rise. Doane's vice president of admissions, Dan Kunzman, said the postcard—which was pulled after the resulting brouhaha—was to get potential applicants "to realize that the state of Nebraska isn't a 300-mile cornfield." Possibly, the University of Nebraska–Lincoln had much the same goal in mind when it agreed to let Mötley Crüe drummer Tommy Lee film his reality show, *Tommy Lee Goes to College*, on campus.

Of course, one could make the case that such outlandish stunts are more likely to repel serious students than attract them. And your urge to rifle through your kid's mail with an eye to steering them away from the cheesiest and sleaziest solicitations is understandable. But wait a second. You might want to make a mental note of schools that appear to actually need quality applicants. Scratch the surface of their sales pitch and you might uncover some genuine opportunity.

Some schools in demographically deprived areas are so serious about attracting good students that they'll incentivize them with valuable academic and financial benefits. Prospective students have been convinced to apply and attend after receiving personal notes from professors discussing internship possibilities and research prospects. Others have been tempted by generous scholarships and attractive work-study programs.

Groucho Marx famously quipped that he didn't want to belong to any club that would accept him as a member. But if your kid is seriously—not frivolously—courted by an underpopulated school, you may want to encourage them to think about the advantages of being in the driver's seat. Ask not what your kid can do for Nebraska, but what Nebraska and its counterparts can do for your kid. Who knows? You might be pleasantly surprised.

SPOTTING A BUYER'S MARKET

Enrollment at the University of Nebraska was down 2 percent in 2004. It dropped nearly 4 percent at the school's flagship Lincoln campus, marking a thirty-year low.

Secret #28

Look on the Sunny Side

In a survey of more than forty-seven thousand students on seventy-four campuses in the spring of 2004, the American College Health Association found that 7.7 percent of those polled suffered from seasonal affective disorder (SAD). The most recognized form of SAD is "winter depression," characterized by recurrent episodes of depressed mood, oversleeping, increased appetite with carbohydrate craving, and weight gain. The symptoms begin in the fall and continue through the winter months.

Light therapy is a SAD treatment with a track record of established-reputation effectiveness. *Ipso facto*, being exposed to more daylight hours may have a preventative effect.

Just for the heck of it, let's pick a random midwinter date—say, January tenth—and at the U.S. Naval Observatory's website, compare times for daylight hours in a few random American cities. If you were going to school in Hanover, New Hampshire (home, as it happens, of Dartmouth College), on that date, you would greet the sun at 7:22 A.M. and bid it adieu at 4:37 P.M. If you were cracking the books in Ithaca, New York (home of Cornell University), you couldn't schedule your morning yoga sun salutes until 7:35 A.M. (and then only if you had your Polartec yoga pants). Cambridge, Massachusetts; Providence, Rhode Island; New Haven, Connecticut? Don't ask. Oh, okay. It's *dark* and it's *cold*. I'm sorry, but you asked.

On the other hand, if one attended college in, say, Austin, San Diego, or Miami, January tenth would be a very different day indeed: warmer *and* brighter (South Florida sunset deferred until 5:48 P.M., thank you). Ah, but would it be better?

Who's to say? Older Americans routinely base choices on where to live, at least in part, on climate and hours of daylight. Would it really be the end of the world if your child was to at least factor in these and other quality-of-life considerations when choosing a spot in which to spend the next four years of their existence?

Of course there's more to a sensible choice of school than weighing relative opportunities to wear shorts on the quad or tan on the dorm roof in December. Looking for a warm school simply because it's temperate is just as silly as aiming for a "hot" school just because it's trendy. But if your child is prone to wintertime blues or simply tends to feel happier and less stressed in a milder clime, why not factor in such personal preferences when helping them search for colleges with all the right criteria for them? They may feel grateful and relieved. You may get to wear shirtsleeves when you pick them up for winter break. And, best of all, you still get to remind them to wear sunscreen.

SUNSHINE IN JANUARY?

If you want a lot of sun, consider going to school at the University of Arizona at Tucson, the University of Denver in Colorado, the University of New Mexico in Albuquerque, or the University of California at San Diego. According to the National Climatic Data Center you'll have a 70 to 80 percent likelihood of clear blue skies—in January.

For the sunniest school in America, enroll at Arizona Western College. It's in Yuma, Arizona, which averages a 90 percent year-round chance of sunshine.

Secret #29
Think Globally

Thinking of sending your kid for a semester abroad? Maybe you should think bigger—say, on a global scale. More and more Americans are obtaining degrees from foreign universities. The educational advantages of cross-cultural learning and, in some cases, foreign language immersion, are ideal preparation for life in a global community and economy. There are practical advantages, too.

Many international undergraduate degrees can be completed in three years. Tuition can be significantly cheaper (Canada's outstanding McGill University cost American students $14,000 for tuition, room, board, and fees in 2005; Australian National University in Canberra cost just under $10,000). And, increasingly, foreign universities are opening more slots to students from other countries (who add diversity and pay higher fees than nationals), so applicants are entering a buyer's market.

It takes a certain kind of student to successfully study abroad for years—more mature and self-directed than some of their peers and more willing to tackle their own laundry, since overseas express mailing of dirty T-shirts gets pretty pricey. It takes a certain kind of parent, too—more willing to endure longer breaks between visits and fewer cell phone chats. But if your child and your relationship are up to it, applying to a foreign school may merit serious consideration. But brace yourself—they may well get in. Then, before you know it, it's time to bid them adieu, ciao, or cheerio. Hold back your tears. It can be their adventure of a lifetime. And if that's not incentive enough, think of the frequent-flyer miles.

FOREIGN BACKUP

Americans are always in a rush, but many foreign universities have deadlines that are substantially later than American counterparts. Many also have rolling admissions in place until the first day of class.

Secret #30

Consider Opting Out

Last year my family and I moved into a new house—well, a new old house. Each time I plugged in my blow-dryer, lights went out all over the upper floor. Each time I attempted to toast a slice of bread, the entire house went dark, though the bread remained light. We needed an electrician.

Ha!

The yellow pages listed several, but our calls either went unanswered or were responded to by minions who could barely contain their giggles as they told us there might be some availability come, say, a year from spring. Finally we threw ourselves on the mercy of a friend at our local hardware store. He spirited us into the storeroom and scribbled down the private cell phone number of an electrician with instructions to share it with no one and to use the code words "Jack sent us."

The electrician arrived and sorted out our wiring. His knowledge and skill were invaluable to us. When he left at the end of the day, I didn't mind at all that I had to pay $1,100. I slept soundly, feeling assured for the first time that our domicile wasn't about to spontaneously combust.

But my electrician had a problem. During a lunchtime chat he told me he was sorry he had no one to whom he could teach his craft. "No one wants to be an electrician," he said. "They all want to go to an academic college."

In this country, we are proud that nearly everyone who wants a college education can get one. That's something to be proud of all right. But it begs some questions: Does everyone *have* to go to college? Are some kids going, not because they want to, but because they feel embarrassed not to? And, finally, if everyone is off getting liberal arts or business degrees, who is going to prevent all of our houses from burning down? And who is going to build those houses in the first place?

I don't mean to sound sacrilegious, but doubtless some of you know a kid—perhaps even yours—who has the interest and aptitude needed to master a valued technical trade that is not necessarily tied to a bachelor's degree or that is perhaps tied to a degree from a college with vocational programs. Would it be so wrong to support them if that seemed like a viable and appropriate option? Somebody has to, if we want to keep the lights on.

THE BEST OF BOTH WORLDS?

At the Wentworth Institute of Technology in Boston, students can earn a bachelor's degree in construction management. Their education readies them to manage large projects or to run smaller carpentry and home-building business. Business and communications skills are taught along with technical skills.

Professors at Wentworth say there are a lot of young people who were B and C students in high school but who shine in this hands-on atmosphere. They point out that 100 percent of their graduates have full-time jobs in construction firms, earning a median salary of $46,000 a year right out of school.

Secret #31

Let the Shoe Fit (A Fairy Tale)

"Knock, knock."

"Who's there?"

"Prince Charming."

"What do you want?"

"I have a very special shoe here. If your kid can get their foot in it, they can go to an elite Ivy League school."

"Well, let me just have that. . . . Ah, it fits."

"Hold on, I need to see for myself."

"Okay,"—*grunt, shove*—"there. See?"

"I'm not sure . . . your child looks somewhat pained."

"Not my kid. This shoe is exactly the right size."

"What's with the limp?"

"Too much soccer practice. My kid always made the travel team."

"What's with the tears?"

"My kid's very compassionate. Must be remembering all that community service."

"I don't know. I'm thinking . . . maybe the wait list."

"No, no, not the wait list! Watch, I'll make my kid dance in these shoes. See? *Tra-la.* How graceful."

"Listen, I don't think she's the one. I'm sorry. But while I'm here, I have this other shoe. Why don't you have her try it? I know it's not as flashy, but it's very comfortable and practical, and if it fits, she can go to a matching school."

"Well, is it a quality shoe and a quality school?"

"Yes, the quality is just as good as the other. Don't get caught up in the designer thing. That's my advice."

"Hmmm. I have to say, that shoe looks pretty smart on her— and she actually seems to like wearing it."

"She'll go far in it. You watch."

And they all lived happily ever after.

Chapter 5: **Testing, Testing, SAT**

Secret #32

SATs Don't Stand the Test of **Time**

I know a man, now in his midforties, who got perfect math and verbal scores on his SAT. I know this about him because he manages to work it into a conversation within ten minutes of meeting anyone for the first time. Knowing about this fellow's high school testing accomplishment leads me to one certain conclusion: He is an idiot.

"Wait," you will protest. "Getting double eight hundreds meant you were really smart, maybe a genius."

To this I'll reply: "If he's so smart, how come his SAT scores are still the defining event in his life?"

This man is a corporate officer whose company org chart shows him about midway up its executive ladder. By most measures you might say he's a success. But every time Mr. Perfect Score talks about his SAT, you can see people wondering: Why hasn't he produced cold fusion, brought peace to the Middle East, or figured out whether Pluto is actually a planet or just some social-climbing hanger-on?

Why, indeed. Because the SAT measures very little other than how good one is at the art of guesswork and at thinking like test-item writers at the ETS. It's no measure of general intelligence, let alone creativity, innovation, adaptability, persistence, vision, passion, *com*passion, humor, or people skills. It certainly doesn't—as Mr. Perfect Score illustrates—mark you as a scintillating conversationalist.

In recent presidential elections, much has been made of candidates' SAT scores, many of which were less than remarkable. Me, I don't necessarily want a commander in chief who has a penchant for guessing. Remember, this is the guy whose briefcase has the nuclear-weapons launch codes in it. How about someone who's really good at, say, diplomacy?

By the way, it's absolutely possible for your kid to get into a good school without *ever* taking an SAT. Fully one-fifth of America's colleges don't require any standardized test scores for entry, and most others will cheerfully accept the ACT—a more straightforward, content-based test—in the SAT's stead. Still, I'll bet you're going to encourage your child to take the SAT, anyway. Because you will want to be on the safe side; because, mostly due to savvy marketing, the SAT has become an American rite of passage; and, finally, because deep down you believe that no child of yours could really want to avoid a good sentence-completion challenge.

Okay, but if they do take the SAT, remember: There's no sense in defining them, or letting them define themselves, by its benchmarks. And no matter how it turns out, if they meet me twenty-five years from now, ask them to *please not tell me about it*.

THE ACT OPTION

Each year, 2.2 million students take the SAT exam. Many could avoid it if they chose to.

Would-be test-takers exploring the ACT option will find several differences between this and the SAT. Among them:

* The ACT includes a science-reasoning section, and its essay section is optional.
* The ACT has no wrong-answer penalty.
* Students taking the ACT can take the test multiple times and then choose which score to submit.

THE NO-TEST OPTION

At Bates College—a very selective but very open-minded institution in Lewiston, Maine—submitting SAT scores has been optional for more than twenty years. The difference in grade point averages between submitters and nonsubmitters, says college vice president Bill Hiss, is five-one-hundredths of a GPA point.

In 2004, one of America's top fifty corporations went to the Bates College campus. They interviewed twenty-seven seniors and offered positions to all twenty-seven.

Endurance Counts . . . or Should

In the belief that anything worth doing is worth overdoing, the new improved SAT is 25 percent longer than the old one—taking nearly four hours to complete. For those of you who may not be so good at the math part, that's nearly 240 minutes or enough seconds to repeat "one-Mississippi" 14,400 times.

That's not four hours interrupted by meetings or phone calls or breaks to check on the stock market or weather.com. It's four hard-core hours of doing plane geometry and data analysis, writing essays, and correcting sentences with misplaced modifiers ("Walking to school to take the long test, my hands started to shake.")

Not to blow my own horn, but I consider myself to be a moderately accomplished person with a fairly wide range of interests. So I decided to make a list of all the tasks that I can carry out successfully for four hours in a row. Here it is:

Things I Can Do Well for Four Hours Straight

1. Sleep

Go ahead, make your own list.

See what I mean? I think these kids ought to be rewarded for pure stamina and for the sheer guts it takes to undertake such an ordeal. After all, as Woody Allen said, 80 percent of success in anything is simply showing up. So, let's see (more math): if the top possible score is now 2,400, then that computes to a score of 1,920 for attendance.

I'm thinking the ETS may not see it this way, but as parents, we can try to compensate. When your kids come home from this protracted ordeal, give them a hug and their favorite snack. Encourage them to take a nap and then let them binge on reality TV. Suppress the desire to ask them how they think they did (they won't know, anyway) and tell them you're proud of them *just for doing it.*

You are, aren't you?

Secret #34

Intelligence **Is More Than** a Quotient

A Supreme Court justice once said of pornography: "We can't define it, but we know it when we see it." Intelligence is much the same. There is that *je ne sais quoi* that bright, curious, and adept people emanate. We all recognize it, yet psychologists disagree as to how to quantify it. Just *quoi* the heck is it?

The prevailing theory, the one that informs the vast majority of IQ and other standardized testing, is that of the G factor. The G stands for "general" intelligence, and the theory contends that intelligence depends on some basic, inherent trait in a person that underlies aptitude in all areas. Okay. But the way this theory has been applied is to assume that this G factor can be ascertained by measuring verbal and mathematical abilities and extrapolating overall mental capacities from those results.

In sharp contrast, a theory of "multiple intelligences" says that intelligence can be viewed as special abilities. Howard Gardner, whose theory it is, says intelligence takes at least seven separate and distinct forms. Mathematical and verbal abilities are two of them. The others are musical, spatial, body movement (of the caliber employed by dancers and athletes), and inter- and intra-personal skills (the latter two comprising what has come to be known as "emotional intelligence").

A former psychology student of mine—a woman accustomed to being labeled an academic whiz based on her impressive math-ematical abilities and strong vocabulary—told me how one of her instructors had truly brought home the meaning of multiple intel-ligences by giving her class an SAT-type exam consisting solely of musical and spatial-intelligence measures. The students' abysmal scores were at once humbling and enlightening.

Let's face it, based on the multiple-intelligence theory, nearly all of us can claim some areas of innate expertise, and nearly all of us simultaneously qualify as dolts. Want to try this at home? Take yourself on a field trip to Ikea and purchase, say, an armoire or a set of bunk beds. Once home, open the box and attempt to assem-ble the five hundred pieces within based on the accompanying in-structions (i.e., three Swedish words and an arrow). There are two kinds of people in the world: those who can do it (the spatially gifted) and the rest of us (sorely in need of spatial education). Whom would you trust to build you a house or lead you out of a dark forest?

A few years back, there was an attempt to incorporate Lego construction and creativity into admissions exams for colleges of engineering and the like. Sadly, the movement seems to have fiz-zled. The good news is that many corporations are integrating Lego testing in management exercises. A team is given an assign-ment to build a structure and finds that a critical piece is missing. Consensus must be reached as to how to proceed. This tests not only spatial thinking, but also resourcefulness and communication and leadership skills.

What I'm getting at here, of course, is that having an impres-sive grasp of synonyms and a knack for logarithms is wonderful. So are many other things—the ability to understand chord structure, to design a building or construct a suspension bridge, to throw a javelin or dance on point, to make people laugh. So, especially, is the ability to do any such things with so much grace as to make them seem effortless.

That, according to my theory, is not the G but the "gee-whiz" factor. If your child has it, let them know how precious it is. Never let anyone tell them different.

Secret #35

Test-Prep Tactics:
Don't Be Shocked

VOCEL, a wireless technology developer, and the Princeton Review, which is a test-prep company, have teamed up . . . They say they're trying to make studying for the SAT a little less onerous. They send you a question as a text message. You respond. And if you get it right, you get [a pleasant pinging sound]. If you get it wrong, the phone vibrates, though VOCEL's CEO Carl Washburn says he really wanted to have it shock you instead.

Morning Edition, National Public Radio, December 21, 2004

Fast-forward to the workplace, 2010.

"Bob, I just don't know about these new hires."

"I know what you mean, Denise. They do seem a bit high-strung."

"I'll say. Take Emily over there. See, the one weeping in the corner. I asked her to proofread a memo, and she, well, she backed away from it like it was radioactive. She kept mumbling something about the horrible things that happen to people who fail to correct all sentence errors."

"That's funny. Juan did practically the same thing when I asked him to run some numbers for me. He seemed agreeable enough at first, but then he wanted to know if I'd included any negative integers. He said negative integers gave him heart palpitations—literally."

"Is that him over there now, with the defibrillator? I have to say he seems a little short of breath."

"Well, when it happened last week, the paramedics said it was just a panic attack. But, still, it gave me pause."

"Really, Bob, it's getting a little difficult to run the shop around here what with all the emotional outbreaks and medical emergencies. I have to tell you, productivity is down."

"Well, let's give them another few weeks to adjust and see how it goes. I hate to terminate them. I mean, they just seem so . . . fragile."

"Do you want to look into that Prozac-in-the-watercooler initiative they're trying over at Omnicorp?"

"You know what, Denise, that's not a bad idea. Not bad at all."

Secret #36

Timing Isn't Everything

Every so often, a toy that reflects a national obsession makes its way into the marketplace . . . This year's example is the Time Tracker, a device whose purpose is to help children improve their performances on . . . standardized tests. Recommend age 4 and up.

—*The New York Times*, December 20, 2004

"Mommy, Mommyyyyyy," shrieked little Cassandra. "Make it stop!"

The shrill siren sound and blinking red light had startled her once again. Unthinkingly, the preschooler had lost track of time while finger painting. She'd grown enchanted with the particular way that the afternoon sun was filtering through the living room drapes and dappling the piece of artwork she was supposed to finish in—what did they say?—twenty minutes. She'd wanted to add a splash more green to the picture, a nice swirl right up there in the corner. But now, of course, it was too late.

Across the street, nine-year-old Matthew was spellbound by a Harry Potter tome. His favorite characters were cornered in a

Hogwarts restroom by a pair of nasty trolls. As usual, he couldn't wait to find out what happened next. In fact, he was so devoted to the books that his teachers often commented on how J. K. Rowling's writing had worked magic on Matthew's reading skills. But, alas, the trolls and young heroes had to wait. The digital readout on Matthew's Time Tracker had set off an electronic male voice booming, "Time's up!" Sighing, the boy put down his book and turned off the device before his parents could scold him.

Around the corner, seven-year-old Robin was practicing piano. She didn't care for scales at all, so she veered off into a little tune she had made up on her own. She liked that one a lot, so she decided to play around with it and try it in another key. She threw in a scale here and there in case her mom and dad were listening. They *were* listening, and smiling. Robin had been at the piano for hours. When the girl looked up later, she'd probably do what she always did, wonder where all the time had gone. Robin's mother lit the oven to keep her daughter's dinner warm a bit longer as the girl played and played.

One of these children is destined for greatness, and it's . . .

Publisher's Note—The author is unable to finish this essay because her time is up. She said she trusted you to figure out the rest.

The Time Tracker, a device aimed at kids to improve standardized test performance, became available in February 2004. By the end of that year, its sales were 30 percent over forecast. Lana J. Simon, spokesperson for the Illinois-based company that manufactures Time Tracker, said the company "had to reorder the product multiple times to meet the demand." Time Tracker retails for $34.95.

Secret #37

Breathe

On the morning of the big exam, send your child off with a final instruction: breathe.

Duh.

I know, breathing seems sort of obvious. Inhale and exhale, right? Taking time out to be put on a respirator can take a real toll on one's score. But I mean *really* breathe—deeply, in order to re-oxygenate the brain and reinvigorate the body.

The SAT has always been physically grueling. At today's length, just shy of four hours, it is torturously so. Human beings, even the most young and lithe specimens, are not meant to sit crunched and hunched for an eighth of a day in wobbly wooden chairs with splintered seats. And wait, did someone say "lumbar support"? You'd get more reclining in a pot of boiled noodles.

Even yoga devotees who routinely contort their bodies into poses meant to resemble everything from cats and cows to bridges and wheels would be hard-pressed to maintain equanimity in "testing pose." After even thirty minutes of sitting in testing posture, muscles ache and physical energy is sapped. The brain is distracted—and who can blame it? It doesn't care what $5(x^4y^5z^6)^3$ equals. It wants ibuprofen and a hot water bottle.

In my humble opinion, every copy of the SAT should come with its own on-site shiatsu masseuse. Until then—and that could be a while—encourage your test-taker to periodically sit tall, inhale deeply into the diaphragm, hold the breath briefly, then exhale slowly (the exhale should last longer than the inhale) while visualizing the column of air being pushed up the spine and out through the crown of the head. Wiggling the fingers and toes and rolling the neck from side to side as a postscript is a good idea, too. All of this will reinvigorate brain, body, and attitude.

Try it yourself.

There, see what I mean?

It may seem ironic that students who can master complex mathematics and challenging vocabulary need to be reminded to breathe. It may seem silly that you yourself need to be reminded. But we all do. We live so much in our heads that we forget that they are inextricably connected to our bodies and that the mind-body system has a wisdom of its own. If understanding this is not a measure of one's "aptitude," I don't know what is.

IN AND OUT

Diaphragmatic breathing is the relaxation technique that has been repeatedly shown to be most effective in reducing test anxiety. Ten deep, slow breaths take a little more than a minute. To help yourself count to ten, you can visualize a birthday cake with ten lit candles. With each breath, picture one of the flames being extinguished.

Ahhhhh.

Secret #38
Sleep on It

What's the best thing for your test-taker to do twenty-four hours before the big one?

Nothing.

At least nothing that has to do with testing. Tell your kid to go to a mall, go to a movie, play music, play tennis, play board games. If they attempt to crack an SAT or ACT prep manual, threaten to disinherit them.

Ten hours before? Nightie night. Give them some hot milk or cocoa. Draw them a bath. Turn on their lava lamp. Draw the shades. If you suspect they've got vocabulary flash cards stashed under their pillow, conduct a purge.

They've done enough, and then some. The unconscious mind—a resource at least as valuable as the conscious one when pivotal moments loom—needs a chance to process what's been happening and gird itself for the task that lies in the immediate future. When it is well-rested, it will do its job—providing those flashes of insight and intuition that seem to come "from nowhere." In such ways are the best hunches played and the most accurate guesses made.

I have no doubt there have been times in your own life when you decided deliberately to sleep on a nagging problem and awoke knowing its solution as if by magic. The same principle applies. Much of what happens in the mind lies below the surface. Teach your child to respect that principle. It will help them do better at standardized test-taking and at really important stuff.

While you're at it, get some shut-eye yourself. Sleep tight.

Secret #39

The New SAT Didn't Kill Anyone

In the spring of 2005, three hundred thousand high school students took the first ever, much-ballyhooed new SAT. It consisted of three eight-hundred-point sections, instead of the previous two such sections, boosting the Holy Grail of the perfect score up to 2,400. There was so much news coverage surrounding the event that one would have thought the world was coming to an end, so much so that even Michael Jackson updates were relegated to the back pages.

The gist of the stories was that everyone was anxious. Kids were nervous about taking a longer test and about handling its new writing section, which tests grammar and usage skills and requires the completion of an essay—preferably a coherent one—in twenty-five minutes. The essay would be graded not by machines but by humans—who could complicate the situation with a degree of subjectivity.

Mostly, however, prospective test-takers were anxious because they would be facing the unfamiliar. When there's a large element of uncertainty, anxiety breeds faster than bunnies. It didn't help that the media kept referring to the test's "maiden voyage." Play word-association with that phrase and you come up with one thing: *Titanic*.

Then, on March twelfth, hundreds of thousands of nervous youngsters sat down and did what they had to do. They scribbled their essays and attempted to discern multiple-choice answers to a slew of language arts, critical reading, and math questions. Then, somehow, it was over. Exit polls showed that students were still uncertain about how it all went, but they were at least relieved that the ordeal was behind them.

In April, the scores came out. A lower percentage of students got perfect scores than usually did on the old test, but no one was certain whether that was because the bar was set higher or because of human essay-scorers or perhaps because even test-prep courses had been fraught with an element of the unknown. Or maybe it was simply due to nerves. The good news for the hardy souls who faced the exam was that college-admissions personnel admitted that they were perplexed as well. It seemed that this once, at least, a less-than-stellar showing on the SAT might not be such a big deal.

The main thing, though, was that the end of the world actually did not occur. In fact, this maiden voyage ended without a single fatality. All who went aboard came ashore and lived to tell the tale. In the future when they speak of it, and they will, their adventure will give them a certain cachet. "Why, yes, young man, I was one of the first to take that danged new SAT—and look at me now."

They'll dine out on it for years, as well they should. First-timers, *bravo*. Live long and prosper.

Of the three hundred thousand students who took the new SAT the first time it was given, 107 got perfect scores.

The average number of students who got a perfect score each time the old SAT was given the previous year was 134.

Flash Card

It's All About Vocabulary—the "S" Words

Scintillating—What you hope your child's essay will be.

Scintilla—How much scintillation you should settle for.

Schizophrenic—What it feels like to try to convince thirteen colleges they are all your number-one choice.

Sacrosanct—What you think the Ivy League is.

Sanguine—How you should feel about your child's chances of admission (that is, *optimistic*).

Salubrious—The effect that being sanguine about college will have on your well-being.

Solecism—Grammatical mistake (avoid on applications).

Solipsism—Belief that one is the center of the universe (avoid in personal statements).

Seraphic—The way parents remember their little angels after they leave for college.

Senility—The reason parents are lucky to remember anything.

Senescent—Old (okay, I'll stop).

Superannuated—Very old (okay, really, I'll stop).

Chapter 6: Activities Are Supposed to Be Fun

Secret #40

Admissions Fads Come and Go

Ken Jennings won an unprecedented seventy-four-game *Jeopardy!* sweep in the summer and fall of 2004. He took home 2.5 million well-deserved dollars and impressed the heck out of millions of TV viewers. We loved Ken. We loved the ease and alacrity with which he moved from subject to subject. We loved his enthusiasm for acquiring a broad range of knowledge. We all wanted to invite Ken to Sunday brunch and talk about this and that.

But if Ken Jennings had applied to an elite school in the fall of '04, he might not have gotten in. Because he was bright and well-rounded. That's why.

I know, I know. Once upon a time, admissions officers relished the thought of filling their halls of learning with bright, well-rounded kids. But then those kids—newly labeled with the pejorative-sounding acronym BWRK—fell from favor. It seems too many parents made the horrible mistake of raising engaged, earnest kids who studied hard, played sports, participated in student government, and perhaps even performed some community service that wasn't on a list of requirements. Now those kids' very well-roundedness is held against them. What colleges prize, says former Duke admissions officer Rachel Toor, are angular kids, those with a sharply focused interest or talent. Renaissance types are out; aficionados are in.

Who knew? If your kid is round, what can you do about their anachronistically spherical shape now? It's too late to inundate them in 24/7 oboe lessons or ship them off to spend their formative years in a research biosphere. There's little hope, at this stage, that they'll be cast in a touring ballet company or be preemptively tapped for a NASA mission.

And what if your kid is angular? Suppose their angle doesn't have quite the incline that their desired college is, well, angling for? "We already have a Sanskrit scholar, thank you. Would you know where we can find a marine paleontologist?"

For better or worse, your kid has been shaped a certain way. College-admissions fads will come and go, but the world needs all kinds of shapes. We need bright, well-rounded people to write, to teach, to doctor, to make law, to make movies, to make money, to make peace between those with opposing points of view. We need them to synthesize, to philosophize, and, goodness knows, to socialize. Who better to liven up a dinner party or raise the bar in a rousing game of Trivial Pursuit?

But we need angular types, too, with angles of all inclinations. We need the dedicated, the devoted, and the obsessive to cure diseases, to make divine music and great art and breakthrough technologies, to explore unknown terrain, to drive humankind to new heights, to make the impossible possible.

Never lament the shape your kid is in, no matter what's in vogue. Don't try to package a circle as a square, or stuff a square peg into a round hole. Let them pursue the things—or the one thing—that thrills them. Just be proud and grateful that they are in pursuit of something.

WORDS OF WISDOM

BWRK = bright, well-rounded kid. Too bad it's become pejorative. So, how about this acronym for your little BWRK?

Beloved = because you cherish them

Well-respected = because just about everyone, other than faddish admissions types, likes and admires them

Keeper = because you're glad you didn't trade them in for an angle

Secret #41

He Who Fences May **Miss** the Point

Middle-class folk wisdom has it that fencing is one of those activities that can make your child different enough to get him or her into that certain college . . . That perception has translated into a boom in high school fencing . . .

—*The New York Times*
October 17, 2004

For a moment I think it's too good to be true. But, hey, this could really work out. I know, I'll borrow my neighbors' pickup, drive to Home Depot, and fill that flatbed full of wooden pickets. For years we've been thinking our front lawn could use a nice, neat enclosure. I can hand my middle schooler a shovel and a mallet. He'll get a head start on the competition, and I'll have the June Cleaveresque yard of my dreams.

Ah, but no. Dang, I knew I shouldn't have finished reading that *Times* article. It turns out they mean, you know, fencing. *En garde. Touché.* And whatever other French-type things sword-wielding swashbucklers say when they're trying to skewer one another in the solar plexus.

I know what's already happening. From Hoboken to Cape May, parents who got up earlier than I did this morning are feverishly booking fencing lessons for their sons and daughters. They're pestering high school principals to start intramural fencing teams. They're browsing the Web for fencing paraphernalia—which, it turns out, includes special jackets, breeches, socks, shoes, masks, gloves, and a potpourri of weapons (weapons!) with assorted blades, grips, and guards. Not that I checked.

Why fencing? Because admissions officers will be impressed by applicants whose saber-slinging skills prove they can think on their feet and react quickly in the moment. Won't they? Well . . . no. Near the end of the article, a university spokesperson maintains, "Fencing does not really stand out more than any other activity in which a student does well." Still, I can't help but wonder: What if *my* son, who seems not entirely to have mastered the concept of opposable thumbs, were to transform himself into a nimble ninja or a zestful Zorro? Would that effort render him Ivy-worthy?

Just then, my boy saunters into the kitchen and reaffirms his inability to crack open a box of Triscuits right end up. I envision John Belushi as Samurai middle schooler. I envision seventh-grade shish kebab. I see fencing scholarships disappearing more quickly than snack crackers.

No matter. Now that everyone and their sister is about to take up fencing, some other activity will become the alleged hot ticket to admissions coups. I turn my head to the window and gaze thoughtfully. Our ragged-edged lawn seems to be crying out to me, and an epiphany dawns. I wonder what time Home Depot opens?

Secret #42

Summer **Sucking-Up** Not Required

A high school sophomore recently called to ask if I thought she should spend the summer at a study program in Brussels or if she should take summer courses at the Ivy League school she longed to attend as a college freshman in a few years' time.

"Would you rather spend your summer in New England or Belgium?" I asked.

"Belgium."

"Where do you think you'd learn more things of interest to you?"

"Belgium."

"Where do you think your experiences might contribute more to your growth?"

"Belgium."

"Okay, and where is the chocolate better?"

That settled it, she said. She was going to Brussels.

But seriously, I explained, I've known many academic achievers who spent a high school summer at their targeted first-choice college and didn't gain entry there as a freshman. I'm sure there's no policy against it, but I don't see how it helps distinguish an application to say, "I've already spent time at your school, and I liked it." Admissions officers already think their school is an excellent place to be. If an application and essay echo that sentiment, they haven't learned anything new about *the applicant*, now, have they?

If your kid is lucky enough to have interesting choices available for summer study, encourage them to choose the one that excites them most. If that happens to involve being at their future target school, fine—just so they know they won't get any suck-up points.

By the way, if your kid doesn't plan to do summer study but needs (and perhaps even wants) to work full time, join a volunteer program, or even work at perfecting their tennis swing, that's beyond okay. Kids who participate in summer study of any kind do not necessarily have an edge. Beware of marketing materials that imply otherwise.

It's summer, for heaven's sake. Tell them to enjoy it. Tell them to follow their bliss. And if they really can't make up their minds about what to do, tell them to find out where the chocolate is better.

Secret #43

Don't Call It Camp

More and more high schoolers are being solicited to spend part of their junior year summer at institutions of higher learning that host college-admissions prep "camps." There, over a two-week period (costing roughly $3,000!), "campers" engage in practice application and essay writing and in SAT prep. They receive guidance on school selection and take numerous field trips to college campuses.

Good idea?

Sure, if you want another profit-driven scheme to pander to the fears of parents who want to give their child a perceived edge.

Don't get me wrong; it's not a bad idea to get started with college planning and applications over the summer. It's great to have the luxury of time to focus without the pressures of school interfering. Kids who start their senior year with a firm idea of where they're applying, with some of their paperwork accomplished, and with an essay or two under their belts will have a much calmer and better-organized fall. Schoolwork, social life, and family life will be all the better for it.

But it's possible to get a jump start on one's own without going to an expensive prep program. A kid who is willing to devote summer days to such efforts at a "camp" can do just as well at home with your help and, if you like, even the help of a private college-admissions counselor. (The summer is when the latter have more free time and less pressure themselves.)

Besides, I'm as suspicious of something called college *camp* as I am of any enterprise that can sell itself only via the use of blatant euphemisms. As George Orwell and George Carlin have shown us, euphemisms are often used by those who market ideas to make unpleasant concepts more palatable ("plus sizes" versus "clothes for the overweight"). Those who contrive euphemisms tend to hold the opinion that those at whom they are aimed are credulous. No, make that gullible. No, make that stupid. (Ah, that's better, isn't it?) Don't validate their belief.

Camp is about canoeing and sailing, making lanyards and bad pottery, toasting s'mores, scratching mosquito bites, short-sheeting your best friend's bunk, and finally managing to swim the entire distance across the lake. Any kid about to go to college is smart enough to know the difference between a *summer camp* and a *wearisome desk-bound curriculum that happens to take place in the summertime*. They know this the same way they will know that *being denied admission* means *being rejected*. Forget college camp and forget warping reality by sugarcoating it in euphemisms. Give your kids their summer back and give them the facts straight up. They'll appreciate your good sense and candor while they're young and impressionable, and they'll remember it until they're senior citizens. Make that elderly. Make that old.

CAMP, MY EYE

If you think your kid would enjoy a fortnight at college camp, here are some camps you might enjoy yourself:

* Tax Prep Camp
* 401K Planning Camp
* Home Equity Loan Camp
* Last Will and Testament Camp

Have fun! And don't forget to write.

Secret #44

Admissions Officers Are **Smarter** Than You Think

I am a college-admissions officer (actually I'm not, but for argument's sake ...). Every day during the admissions season, I'm obliged to pore over dozens of applications, complete with "brag sheets" of extracurricular activities. My job is demanding, and goodness knows I have family and community obligations outside of it. Plus, once in a while, I like to floss, or nap, even. So here's what I want to know: Where does every applicant to my school find the hours to participate in sixty-three clubs, teams, squads, societies, organizations, and associations—and still have time left for enough community service to make Mother Teresa look like a piker?

Oh, I know! They've given up on sleeping and eating. Good, because that makes them the kind of freshmen we're seeking— pie-eyed, jittery, sleep-deprived. Goodness knows our mental-health counselors don't have enough to do. Plus, just think: If these kids' appetites remain so spartan, we'll save a bundle on dining-hall fare.

So, Jessica P.—choir, mentoring society, student newspaper,

Future Doctors of America, Future Lawyers of America, chess team, cheerleader, field hockey, ice hockey, wrestling club, future insider trader, Big Sisters, Meals on Wheels, Future Astronomers, fire drill squad, AV squad, assistant principal's undercover lunchroom double agent—you're in!

Lucas K.—soccer team, school orchestra (first piccolo), lacrosse, first-aid squad, sewing circle, Read-to-White-Collar-Convicts Club (treasurer), student council (president), vice squad (vice president), future engineers, science fair runner-up, Search for Extraterrestrial Intelligence summer internship—likewise!

If only I, as a youngster, had had the fortitude, the stamina, and the personality disorder needed to prepare myself for life in such rigorous fashion. If only I'd had parents who ignored my accelerating gauntness and darkening under-eye circles and who did not wonder why I—who could not carry a tune in a Vuitton bag—had such undying devotion to glee club.

Ah, but then I might have the job I have today, a job where most people assume I'm an imbecile who can't figure out when they're racking up achievements that have nothing to do with their real interests. A job where no one thinks I notice that they're stretched as thin as a sausage skin on an elephant's trunk. A job where people like Jessica P. and Lucas K. don't know I was only kidding when I said they were in.

On second thought, I'm happy with my life just the way it is. And now, my nap.

A BUST FOR BUSY BEES

According to a 2003 report by the National Association for College Admission Counseling, only about 7 percent of colleges place considerable importance on extracurricular activities, including volunteer work.

WHAT ABOUT AP CLASSES?

Despite pressures to take lots of AP (advanced placement) classes in high school, a large University of California, Berkeley study says doing so won't necessarily equate with a resulting academic boost in college. However, students who complete the tests offered at the end of AP courses do tend to improve their college performance.

The AP exams are graded on a scale of 1 to 5. Most colleges grant college course credit for the course only if a student scores 3 or higher. Very selective schools may require a 4 or 5.

So, how many AP courses should a student take? Only as many as they think they can realistically take the exam for and do well in. An overload is counterproductive.

Chapter 7: Essays Don't Have to Be **Perfect**

Secret #45

Meaning of Life **Not** Required

Do you know the story of the young man determined to discover the meaning of life? He climbed and climbed the Himalayas until he found a reclusive yogi who'd spent countless years in deep contemplation. The young man asked the sage his question, to which the yogi replied, "Life is a flower."

"It *is?*" asked the young man.

"You mean, it's *not?*" asked the yogi.

The point: It isn't easy to provide answers to life's most profound questions, and no one writing a college-application essay ought to try.

I know you're nervous about your child's college essay. Somewhere along the line you, and they, got the idea that it could be a critical tipping factor in the admissions process. Here's the real deal: Students place far more emphasis on their personal essays than admissions officers do. It's more realistic to see the essay as *somewhat* important (the category where most admissions officers placed it in a national survey). That said, a truly awful essay could serve as a cold shower on even the hottest and heaviest admissions romance.

What makes for an awful essay? Overreaching is generally the fatal flaw. No admissions officer wants a high school senior to impart the secret of life to them. So, if you or your child think *you* know that secret, you would be well advised to keep it to yourselves.

Similarly, if there's a heretofore-unmentioned black sheep amongst your kin or some other deep, dark secret you've never imparted to your child before, spilling your guts for essay fodder won't help their cause. Leave your family skeletons in the closet where they belong. Nobody likes a tattletale.

Finally, forget about the theory that personal tragedy makes for great essays. Admissions officers are sick and tired of eighteen-year-olds vying to out-tragedy one another. Besides, you really don't want to end up having an argument with your kid about whether you've neglected to provide them with sufficient amounts of misery and misfortune. Those are not pretty conversations.

Still want to help your kid with their essay? That's fine. Surveys show most applicants *do* get some form of help, and admissions officers have come to expect that someone will oversee this aspect of the application. But if you want to tell them something useful, tell them this: Think small; stay humble. Don't use a semicolon unless you know what it's for. And forget the spell-checker. That's why God made mothers.

TIME-MANAGEMENT ALERT

Revising ad infinitum? According to a survey by the National Association for College Admission Counseling, 49 percent of students ranked the essay as a very important part of their application, while only 36 percent of admissions officers agreed.

Secret #46

Honesty Is the **Best** Policy

Few things strike greater fear in the heart of a child—or a parent—than a threat that some infraction of school rules will go on a student's "permanent record." Having a document out there indelibly chronicling each youthful transgression in excruciating detail *(ran in the halls . . . snickered during health ed . . . forgot gym clothes twice in one marking period)* seems to portend doom.

College-application time offers an excellent opportunity to mine this deep-seated Kafkaesque dread. How much will prospective schools be told? How far back will they delve? As far back as that sixth-grade field-trip fiasco? What about the infamous Play-Doh and bite-plate episode?

Relax. Minor indiscretions, no matter how serious an irate biology teacher can make them sound (and you'd be irate, too, if you had to deal with that many liberated frogs), won't serve to bar the doors of higher education to your wayward offspring. Deliberate cover-ups, on the other hand, are never good ideas (ask any white-collar criminal). In the rare case that an infraction resulted in an actual school suspension or expulsion, it's wise to provide details should an application ask for them. Assuming there have been rehabilitative efforts, a reasoned explanation of human fallibility shouldn't cause the sky to fall.

In January 2005, the *New York Times* "Ethicist" column recounted the story of a young woman who was caught sharing test answers with four others in their sophomore year of high school. She was suspended. Even though the record was later expunged (her first offense was her last, and her subsequent behavior and grades were exemplary), she revealed the suspension to her first-choice early decision school—and got in, anyway.

Now don't go overboard. There's no need to start dredging up minor misdeeds to which your child can confess. Admissions officers will get awfully blasé awfully fast if everyone starts sending in essays filled with remorse about feeding peanut butter to the cat. Nevertheless, if something of a more weighty nature occurred, honesty is truly the best policy. Remind your kid that college offers a fresh start. Remind them to take advantage of the opportunity this blank slate offers. While you're at it, remind them to leave their Play-Doh and peanut butter behind. There's no point in courting temptation.

Secret #47

Nobody Likes a **Whiner**

Not since the Greeks made it an art form has tragedy been so in vogue. The college-application essay has made it so. But for better or worse, genuine tragedy seems to be in relatively short supply—unless you count as tragic the number of times college applicants have lamented the lack of disaster, catastrophe, misfortune, and heartbreak in their lives.

I am not exactly certain how the notion that recounting a heartrending story equated with a surefire admissions advantage came into being. Maybe it was that episode of *Felicity* where one of the characters attributed his admission to a selective New York school to his essay on the death of his little brother. (He had no little brother, he later admitted to his girlfriend.)

Thankfully, most applicants wouldn't dream of going so far as to manufacture a bogus tragedy out of whole cloth. On some level, you've just got to know it's bad karma. Not all ends justify all means. Nevertheless, many have taken to trumping up incidents in their lives that can truly be characterized as no more than somewhat discouraging or lightly disruptive and presenting them as full-blown calamities.

In case your child is wondering, none of the following events (or anything remotely resembling them) qualifies as a tragedy:

* My dog (cat/horse/gerbil) almost died but pulled through.
* I can't seem to save enough for a car (sailboat/Harley-Davidson).
* I broke out with hives (acne/poison oak) right before the junior prom.
* The girl/boy I really like doesn't especially like me.
* My parents don't always understand me.
* I tried out for *American Idol* and Simon mocked me.

Making a mountain out of a molehill doesn't make one look like an interesting candidate; it makes one look like a whiner. Put yourself in the shoes of the person who is reading essay after essay. If you were they, wouldn't you tire of complainers? Wouldn't a nice upbeat perspective on life—one that looks on the bright side and even exhibits a wee bit of gratitude for all the things that have gone right—be refreshing?

If your child has overcome some debilitating obstacle or onerous turn of events in their life, of course it's all right to convey that truth. Even so, it's the overcoming of the obstacle that should be the focus.

In application essays, it's best to portray the glass as half full. Or, for a change, perhaps even brimming over.

Secret #48

Save Something for **Oprah**

More on honesty. Sometimes when stress is high, we feel the urge to unburden ourselves to a stranger. You've probably experienced this phenomenon yourself. Ever been stuck in an elevator and told a fellow stuckee your deepest dreads and aspirations? "If I ever get out of this elevator, I'm going to quit my job, cash in my 401K, and hot-air-balloon across Antarctica." Ever confessed your wrongdoings to a fellow passenger on an especially turbulent flight? "And then there was the time I put ants in my little brother's ear."

Well, your child just might feel a similar urge to "tell all" to the anonymous recipient of their college essay. This compulsion may just result in essay topics such as these:

* That time I said my ferret ate my homework—well, I don't actually have a ferret.
* That time I missed my math test because I was sick, I wasn't really that sick.

- My friend Josh is applying to your school, too, and he's smarter.
- Some of my SAT points came from lucky guesses.
- I hate these personal essays like the plague.

If your child feels the need to bare their soul, get them a counselor or a clergyman. But do not—repeat, do not—encourage them to spill their beans to a virtual stranger. Certainly the person reading their essay is not their enemy, but neither is that person their new best friend. Openness is commendable, discretion is more so. Encourage them to strike a balance between not saying anything and saying too much. If that doesn't work, remind them that if they tell all now, they'll have nothing left to tell Oprah later.

Secret #49

One Can Be TOO Politically Correct

Some schools require an essay in which a student must take a stand on an issue. Encourage your child to say what they think, even if it's not exactly (or remotely like) what you think. The application essay is supposed to be a glimpse into the student's mindset and weltanschauung, so don't worry if your child's essay reflects their "true self" or takes an unusual stand. That's the whole point.

Keep in mind that there's no need for your kid to pander to political correctness. Why? Because doing so doesn't say anything about the essay's writer. PC is nothing if not impersonal.

With that in mind, please note this list of things no admissions officer needs to hear from your child, even if such sentiments are deeply heartfelt by them, by you, or by your entire extended family:

1. I'm for world peace.
2. People should just get along.
3. I like the environment.

4. The whole global warming thing makes me nervous.
5. Money isn't everything.
6. I respect all religions and cultures.
7. Native Americans have a right to be peeved.
8. Education is commendable.
9. Endangered species should be unendangered.
10. The underprivileged should have more privileges.

Essay writers, and their parents, should assume that most essay readers, while not exactly likely to rebut any of the foregoing sentiments, won't be enlightened by them either. "World peace—why, I never thought of that!" More important, they won't be engaged, entertained, or educated in any way about who's on the other end of the application.

Forget the cookie-cutter stuff. Let your kid serve the admissions officer a cookie they can chew on.

Secret #50

Imperfection Is **Better**

Is it possible for a personal essay to be too perfect? In a word: indubitably. Er, make that yes. Again, the essay is supposed to be a personal statement. It's supposed to read like a kid wrote it—personally.

A treatise overstuffed with highfalutin vocabulary words will leave a reader not only cold, but also a tad suspicious. "Who came up with this thing, a seventeen-year-old or the undersecretary of state?" Similarly, a piece so technically seamless and intellectually profound that it could have been penned by Susan Sontag will prompt a raised eyebrow. Yes, it *might* have been written by the applicant, but keep in mind that these days, an admissions officer who truly wants to know if this is likely can easily look up that applicant's score on the SAT writing section. If the two don't add up, well . . . it doesn't *necessarily* prove anything, but it makes one wonder.

Many parents are hiring professionals to help their kids formulate and edit their essays. Even if they don't hire a pro, a zealous English teacher or helpful friends and relations may rush in brandishing a red pen and a thick thesaurus. Most students polled say they have had some help with their essay, and that's not unexpected or looked upon askance. Giving an essay a bit of polish is one thing, whereas buffing it to a blinding sheen will detract from its viability.

The person who should have the very final edit on the personal essay is the essay's owner. Ask your kid to go off into their room and read it aloud. Does it sound like something they would say? Does it sound remotely like the way they would say it if asked to do so extemporaneously? If not, it's back to the drawing board. The point of the essay is neither to bedazzle the reader with impeccable stylistic flourishes nor to overwhelm the recipient with multisyllabic synonyms. It's to give decision makers something to hold on to—an image of a real person on the other side of the process, a person who has something to say, even if they say it imperfectly.

FUNNY YOU SHOULD ASK

Should a kid attempt to be funny in their personal essay? Sure, if they are funny. If they don't know by now if they're funny, they're not.

Flash Card

It's All About Vocabulary—the "O" Words

Onerous—The prospect of summarizing eighteen years of life in one tiny application.

Omniscient—What we wish we were so we wouldn't have to wait for acceptance or rejection letters.

Officious—That guy with the attitude in the financial aid office.

Obtuse—That guy with the attitude in the financial aid office.

Obsequious—The way we behaved toward the officious, obtuse guy.

Oblivious—The way he reacted to our reaction.

Occam's razor—The scientific and philosophical rule that simple explanations should be preferred to complex ones. Not applicable to the college-admissions process.

Onomatopoeia—Ow!

Secret #51

Apply to Fewer Schools

There are two things wrong with throwing some spaghetti at the wall and seeing how much sticks. First: *eeewww*, it's gross. Second: nothing may stick at all. There's a chance the spaghetti will just ooze and slither its way to the floor, one painstaking strand at a time.

Yet the throw-spaghetti-at-the-wall approach to college admissions is on the rise, with more and more students hedging their bets by submitting over a dozen applications. At upper-end public and private high schools, twenty applications is a number that one hears with increasing frequency. It's a nice, round number—one college application for each finger and toe. Even in less competitive and anxiety-prone settings, kids who might typically have submitted three or four applications in the past are now up to six or eight.

Do more applications increase the chances of acceptance? One might think so, but one ought to think again.

What's the better way to look for a job?

a. E-mail out a hundred résumés to listings on a website

b. Target three organizations that you believe in and to whom you have something to offer

What's the better way to meet a potential mate?

a. Hand out your phone number to everybody on the crosstown bus

b. Ask three friends if they know anyone with whom you might hit it off

As the architect Mies van der Rohe's dictum has it: less is more. Mies and his Bauhaus contemporaries worked hard at simplifying. They had to, because simplifying is hard work.

Selecting three or four desirable and realistically matched schools is hard work as well. Anyone can fling noodles. The difference shows up in the applications themselves, and in the follow-up contact that students who have chosen schools with careful deliberation have time to conduct. Admissions officers can tell who threw the spaghetti. No, really, they can. If they're reading the eighteenth of nineteen applications a student has filled out, its quality—or lack thereof—sets a tiny little pasta alarm off in their heads.

Encouraging your kid to be judicious about the number of applications they submit will probably help them get in and help keep all of you sane. In the big picture, it will also make an ever-so-small-but-every-little-bit-counts dent in the entire college-admissions hysteria syndrome. That's because the greater the number of extraneous applications filed by students who are cynically shooting for the moon or playing it super-hyper-ultra-safe (or both), the more chaotic and skewed the entire system becomes.

So do yourselves and everyone else a favor: simplify, simplify.

Help your child hone their choices. Pare them down, then pare them again. Remember, always, that less is more. Take it from Mies.

PILES OF PAPER PASTA

In 1993, only 9 percent of students applied to six or more colleges, according to the UCLA Higher Education Research Institute. By 2003, one in five was doing so.

THINKING SMALL

Carl Ahlgren, a director of college counseling who's worked at top-drawer private schools, ran an informal study correlating the number of applications filed with admission success. The students with the highest rate of admission turned out to be those who applied to three schools or fewer. Those with the lowest applied to over eleven.

Secret #52

A Calendar Is an **Anti-Nag** Device

When it comes to large undertakings, salvation is in the details. One way you can assist your aspiring applicant is to help them organize a calendar of what's due when. Application and financial-aid deadlines have a way of sneaking up on you, as do separate high school cutoffs for items like letters of recommendation requests.

The thing about a calendar, of course, is that one needs to check it. Try taping it to the most frequented spot in the household: the fridge. Even at that, backups are a good idea, since the more stressed we are, the more we tend to ignore what's right in front of us. (Remember that time you drove through the garage door?) High-tech types can program PDAs to beep or play tunes when a critical deadline looms; low-tech types can slap Post-it notes on the bathroom mirror (take them down when the deadlines have passed to prevent shaving and makeup mishaps).

Your kid may find your obsession with due dates mildly annoying, but tell them to think of it this way: A calendar is an anti-nag device. It helps you know when it's really important to pester your child and when you, and they, can slack off.

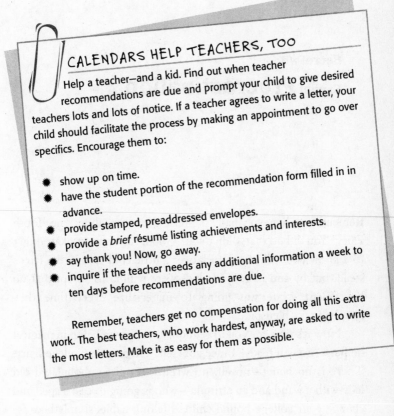

CALENDARS HELP TEACHERS, TOO

Help a teacher—and a kid. Find out when teacher recommendations are due and prompt your child to give desired teachers lots and lots of notice. If a teacher agrees to write a letter, your child should facilitate the process by making an appointment to go over specifics. Encourage them to:

* show up on time.
* have the student portion of the recommendation form filled in in advance.
* provide stamped, preaddressed envelopes.
* provide a *brief* résumé listing achievements and interests.
* say thank you! Now, go away.
* inquire if the teacher needs any additional information a week to ten days before recommendations are due.

Remember, teachers get no compensation for doing all this extra work. The best teachers, who work hardest, anyway, are asked to write the most letters. Make it as easy for them as possible.

Secret #53

Expect Procrastination

Remember when you had to break the news about the Tooth Fairy? You did do that, didn't you? Good. And it went okay, didn't it? I know you still had to fork over a little cold cash in the fairy's stead, but by and large, your kids were willing to accept that no benevolent sprite was going to materialize every time they coughed up a bicuspid.

Now it's time for you to relinquish your own belief in magical helpers. Are you ready? Brace yourself: There is no College Fairy. There is no being—no elf, no wizard, no discombobulated old lady with a wand and an attitude—who is going to cast a spell and change your college-bound child's lifelong habits simply because that child is in the midst of the application process.

I know you've been waiting. One day, you imagine, your legendary little procrastinator will awaken reborn with a newfound zeal to file all of his applications well ahead of deadline. One day—soon!—your winner of the Most Illegible Cursive Award will mend her ways and master perfect penmanship, filling those teeny tiny application boxes with flawlessly dotted *i*'s and crossed *t*'s. Any time now, the College Fairy will *wink, blink, zap* and liberate your wayward offspring from whatever irksome character quirk you imagine stands between them and admissions triumph.

But no. As much as you've been trying to deny it, you already know the truth, don't you? You figured it out on your own, just as your kids figured out that one guy in a sleigh was probably unable to circumnavigate the globe, breaking and entering and dispensing toys to one and all in a single evening. There's no magical intervention on the horizon. Your kid is the same kid they've always been up until now. The only thing that's changed is your level of expectation. You need to wave your parenting wand and zap yourself.

Your procrastinator has always pulled things off before, hasn't he? No matter how unlike your approach, his style of putting off important things—yes, even critical things—until the last minute seems to work for him. This is how he's going to apply to college. Your won't-stay-in-the-lines scribe is going to do nothing whatsoever to improve her handwriting for her applications. She'll scratch in her hieroglyphics just as she has always done.

Can you overnight-mail those last-minute applications? Sure. Is it cheating to decipher and neatly recopy your scribbler's responses? Nah. Just as you filled in the cash gap left by the Tooth Fairy, you may need to do a little ad hoc magic this time around. It may not be exactly the fairy tale you had in mind, but it's extremely likely you'll all live happily ever after.

SOMETHING IN COMMON

Over two decades ago, several private colleges got together and developed an application they unilaterally agreed to accept in lieu of their own customized applications. This caught on, and now hundreds of colleges accept the Common Application. A major advantage is that there will be less paperwork overall if a student fills out one application and sends copies to several schools. But—and there's always a bit of a but, isn't there?—keep in mind:

* Some schools do require a supplemental application to accompany the Common Application.
* Some schools do seem to have a bit of a preference for their own application, even if they don't say so explicitly. Your child should check with their counselor for specifics.

Secret #54

Murphy Wasn't Kidding . . .

So Be **Prepared**

No one knows exactly who Murphy was, though almost everyone knows him as the eponymous author of Murphy's law. Actually, it was three laws:

1. Nothing is as easy as it looks.
2. Everything will take longer than you think it will.
3. If anything can go wrong, at some time it will.

Every year thousands of colleges process thousands and thousands of admissions applications. Not a one of those venerable institutions has proved Murphy wrong yet, and none are likely to.

Odds are, at least one of the schools you so carefully selected will give you pause as they garble your child's name (which we may also assume was carefully selected), not to mention their address, date of birth, social security number, and gender. Grade transcripts, test scores, and those painstakingly gathered teacher recommendations will vanish into the ether with much the same frequency as the socks that vaporize in the dryer. Long periods of silence will be punctuated by horrifyingly inaccurate communiqués, such as a letter from the art department asking your would-be business major why they haven't yet received his watercolor portfolio. Oh yeah, and if anybody in an admissions office is eating lunch at their desk, they'll drop a piece of bread, peanut butter side down, on your kid's essay.

Such snafus will make you somewhat less crazy if you accept that a certain number of them are going to happen. Be prepared. Print hard copies of anything that you submit electronically. Use delivery confirmation for snail mail. Make sure your application fee check has actually been cashed. Check on the status of applications over the Internet where you can. And if you speak to anyone in the admissions office, get a name—well, not just any name, preferably that of the person you speak to.

Will doing all this ensure that Murphy's dogma plays no part in your kid's admissions process? Well, no. But it will make you feel better and will quite possibly help with damage control. That's something. On the other hand, don't get overly complacent. The thing that goes wrong probably won't be the one you most anticipate, but the one you couldn't possibly conceive of in a million years. I don't think Murphy said that, but he should have. Maybe he did, and it just got lost in the mail.

Secret #55

Take Advantage of **Rolling** Admissions

Is your eager applicant thinking about making an early decision? Okay, but as you probably know, getting in means there's no turning back, even if your kid changes their mind about what or where they'd like to study. It also means you won't be able to compare various financial-aid packages. Perhaps worst of all, from an emotional standpoint, if they don't get in early but get deferred into an even larger applicant pool, they may have to endure the indignity of being rejected not once, but twice.

Applying early to a school with rolling admissions, on the other hand, offers a number of practical and emotional advantages. If an applicant gets in and is pleased with their choice, they're done. If they get in but still want options, they can continue applying elsewhere knowing they're secure. If they apply and don't get in, they've lost nothing and, if they like, can add another rolling admissions school to their target list.

I've known some kids who simply didn't want to endure the stress of applying to multiple schools and so picked one that appealed to them and that also had a rolling admissions policy. A timely yes equated to instant gratification and an amazing sense of relaxation. While many of their classmates were still caught in the throes of application hysteria, they thoroughly enjoyed their senior year. I can think of worse ways to go, can't you?

LET'S ROLL

Rolling admissions can be employed as a way to wrap things up early, but it can also be used as a way for students to take a bit more time with the process and to make sure they're making the right choice. They can also be a saving grace in the spring if other options have not panned out.

One caveat: While this process can create less stress in terms of deadlines, other deadlines—such as standardized testing dates—still need to be considered. Also, the later one waits, the less financial aid becomes available.

MORE WORMS FOR THE EARLY BIRD

Another way to resolve things sooner rather than later is by applying for early action. Unlike early decision plans, early action acceptances are not binding. The applicant can still weigh other offers, but they will have the peace of mind that accompanies an early yes.

Secret #56
Don't Send Props

A young man sends a shoe along with the college application. His letter says he wants a foot in the door. A young woman sends a life-sized cutout of herself. Why, it's almost as if she were on campus already! A young scholar with a penchant for woodworking sends a sample of his craft, a handmade faux Shaker chair, delivered FedEx.

Why, oh why, didn't their parents stop them?

Across America, admissions officers cringe when applications arrive accompanied by oversized Jiffy bags and plywood crates. *Now what?* they wonder as the UPS guy wedges his way through their growing piles of self-promoting paraphernalia. The job used to have some dignity; now their office looks like a Costco returns department on the day after Christmas.

Moms, dads, listen: If you notice your children heading to the post office lugging an oversized package and looking smugly pleased with themselves, do everything in your power to intervene. This is one of those moments when playing the parental prerogative card is allowed. Make sure that package is not addressed to any college that might otherwise have actually accepted your offspring. If it is, be firm. *They're not leaving the house with that thing or they're grounded.*

Your insistence on saving your overzealous children from themselves, by the way, should also extend to vetting the paper on which they send in any cover letters, essays, or other written material. No hot pink. No bright yellow. No patterns. No, no, no. Just plain white 8.5 × 11 inch paper. Fold. Put in normal-sized envelope. Add stamp. That's it. Any admissions application accompanied by a gimmick immediately has a strike against it.

Is it nice that these kids are thinking creatively? Sure. They should feel free, in their spare time, to paint, sculpt, compose music, or design freelance point-of-purchase end cap displays for Wal-Mart. But there is a time and a place for all things.

What's that you say? The blow-up doll was *your* idea. Ah, well, I assume you won't make that mistake again. But just in case you were thinking about it, you're grounded.

MAILBAG

Actual items sent to Harvard admissions officers:

* bread, cake, cookies, roses
* a Harvard shield made of chocolate
* photos of an applicant writing his essay with his foot
* copies of an applicant's corrected school papers, since kindergarten
* a stuffed squirrel from an applicant who was also an amateur taxidermist (the dean of admissions said it "spent too much time in the U.S. mail")

Secret #57

Send Videotapes with Caution

You know those reams of old videos you have in the basement, the ones that chronicle your child's first face-in-the-cake birthday bash, their first day of kindergarten, their Halloween costumes, their yearly departures for and returns from camp, and so on? Ever think about commissioning a professional to craft them into a full-scale biographical epic and then sending it off to admissions officers? If so, I know a nice padded suite you might want to spend some time in.

When you hear—as you will—about the up-and-coming admissions video trend, please pay attention to the many caveats that accompany such submissions. It all started when a few high school athletes, hoping to gain the attention of a particular college's basketball, football, volleyball, or lacrosse coach, began stringing together impressive clips that showed them at their best. The tactic sometimes worked. Certain coaches became enthused and, within the policies of their schools, were able to bring some positive influence to bear on admissions decisions. Since then, a few department chairs in areas such as drama, dance, and music have also agreed to screen videos of aspiring student artists. Another college-admissions cottage industry was born, and some video pros began to specialize in productions for the college-bound.

But a word of caution: A video may help your child's cause, but only if they fall into either the sports or arts aspirant category. Even then, serious ground rules apply. Never send such a video without locating the exact person who would be interested in it and obtaining their agreement to view it. Limit the video to a brief—two- to three-minute—clip of relevance. Finally, do not—I repeat, do not—run a *Chariots of Fire* or *Rocky* soundtrack in the background. If you don't know why, please visit the aforementioned padded suite. Enjoy your stay.

Secret #58

Anxiety Can Make You **Careless**

Needles to say . . . I sincerely hope you will except my application.

If you're anything like me, you're most likely to trip up on little things when big things are making you anxious. It's when I get preoccupied with life's large concerns that I tend to leave important papers in library Xerox machines, start down the driveway with my handbag atop the car roof, and neglect what the police consider to be somewhat important traffic hints (e.g., red lights and NO LEFT TURN signs).

Oh, and sometimes I forget to proofread.

If you've been helping your child through the college-application process, you've most likely been looking at the big picture—the "whole enchilada" of grades, recommendations, essays, test scores, and the like. But just as one little thing—for instance, too much hot sauce—can have quite a deleterious impact on an enchilada, small matters can undermine an application into which you and your child have put a prodigious amount of effort.

So, before you send anything out, stop, relax, breathe, and proofread. Do it *without* the help of a word-processing program. Such a program will never find fault with a sentence like "Please except my application," because *except* is, after all, a correctly spelled word—never mind that it may well drive an overworked admissions officer to fits of inconsolable grief, rage, or giggles that border on manic hysteria.

I know you want to get the darned applications in the mail or press the SEND button and be done with them. But, please, re-mind your child to get a good night's sleep and look at them just one more time with a clear head in the morning. You'll be glad you did, or at least relieved, because, I promise you, before you're done, you are 99.9 percent likely to locate, and gleefully correct, quite a blooper.

Maybe not, though. Maybe your kid never makes spelling or punctuation errors. Or maybe you were savvy enough, and cool, calm, and collected enough, to spot every one of them with an initial cursory glance. If this is the case, you're not much worse off for having made certain. But if you're unhappy about having taken the time to be prudent, please except my apology.

PRINT IT OUT

If your child is submitting an application online, urge them to print it out for proofreading purposes. Studies show we tend to catch one-third more errors when we proof a hard-copy document.

Secret #59

Resist the Urge to Write a Clever Letter

Dear Admissions Officer:

I am writing to you about my boy, Chip. In addition to the information in his application and essay, there are a few things I thought you should know about the Chipper:

- *New and Improved—That's right. Chip's always been a good kid, but recently he's become absolutely super.*
- *30 Percent More—Chip weighs at least 30 percent more now than he did when he first started high school. And he's, er, 30 percent smarter, too.*
- *Fresher Scent—It took some doing, but Chip's mom and his gym teacher have been working on this one for years. Trust me, it's much better than it was.*
- *Certified Organic—Chip is pesticide and chemical-free. We had him checked.*

- **Satisfaction Guaranteed**—*I personally guarantee you'll be satisfied with Chip or . . .*
- **Money-back Guarantee**— *. . . if not, you can send me back all the tuition money, and we'll just forget the whole thing.*

Thank you for your consideration.

Sincerely,

"Big Chip" Blodgett III

P.S. **Free shipping**—*Act now, and we'll personally drive Chip to your campus gates. Really. Right away.*

Flash Card

It's All About Vocabulary—the "U" Words

Unctuous—The kind of cheesy marketing letters some colleges send out.

Umbrage—What you have a right to take at such marketing letters.

Ubiquitous—Something that seems to be everywhere, like lists of the "hottest colleges."

Uninformed—What you don't want to be when sifting through the lists.

Unmanageable—What the admissions process will be like for those who believe everything they read.

Unobtrusive—What you want to be during your kid's campus tours.

Secret #60

Reach Out and Touch **Someone**

(But Don't Poke Them in the Eye)

In recent years, a student's "demonstrated interest" has been identified as an issue of rising prominence in admissions decisions. Although there is no standardized way to compute this factor, examples of demonstrated interest include campus visits, contact with the admissions office, and letters of recommendation that stress why the student has a preference for that institution and why they are truly a good fit. National Association for College Admission Counseling data says that 33 percent of institutions consider the student's interest when making an admissions decision. Thirty percent assign this factor moderate or significant importance.

The point is that schools want students who want them. This helps their yield rate—the number of students it actually enrolls out of the number it accepts. But there's an emotional element here as well. Admissions officers are like all people: They want to know that their jobs matter. They want their work to have a positive impact. It can't hurt to encourage your child to reach out in a sincere, friendly manner to a school that genuinely interests them. This doesn't mean inviting the admissions officer to dinner, or even brunch. Don't encourage your kid to write them a song or a sonnet. But do advise them to be personable without getting personal. It might help them get in, and even if it doesn't, it will put them in a better frame of mind.

Secret #61

The Chauffeur's Creed

So, it's time for the campus visit. It's an excellent idea, and an indispensable part of searching for a good-fit school. Actually setting foot on a campus can instantly tell a kid a lot more than poring over a school's website and catalogue for months on end. It affords a potential applicant the opportunity to learn what life is like at a school, straight from the horse's mouth, so to speak, instead of from hearsay and hype. Most important of all, it gives them the "feel" of the place.

But what role does your child want *you* to play during the campus visit? Tireless advocate? Interrogator? Undercover agent? Nah. In most cases they just want you to be their chauffeur. Any query you pose to an administrator, instructor, or—heaven forbid—a student will cause your offspring to cast their eyes skyward, edge away from you as if you have a contagious rash, and assume that I-never-saw-that-person-before-in-my-life posture you've doubtless come to know only too well during their adolescent years.

So be it. The chauffeur role is one you've come to play with flair and, I'm quite sure, can execute perfectly. You've spent much of the last seventeen or eighteen years ferrying your children from Gymboree and Mommy 'n' Me to music, tennis, and skating lessons, to fill-in-the-blank-ball practice, to school dances, to SAT prep classes. But if you've ever watched *Sabrina* (either version), you know, of course, the chauffeur's secret: A good driver keeps their mouth shut and their eyes and ears wide open.

Let your kid do the talking on the campus visit. If you like, you can discuss with them ahead of time some possible questions to pose. Don't pooh-pooh their concerns. "What do you do for fun?" is a perfectly valid concern.

While they're talking and listening, you should be busy observing—not only at the sights and sounds around you, but, even more so, at your child's reaction to what they are seeing and hearing. Be emotionally alert. What expression is your child wearing? No one knows how to read them better than you, and there's no better time than now to read cover to cover.

The drive home allows plenty of time for debriefing, but don't rush it. Let the mood of the day sink in for a while, and then ply your ever-hungry teen with hearty roadside diner fare. Ask them what they liked and disliked about the school. Keep them talking (order another milkshake if you have to) and you keep listening and observing. In *Sabrina*, the astute chauffeur made millions from stock tips that wafted up from the backseat. The information you get from handling the campus visit with chauffeurlike decorum will also prove of immense value.

WHEN TO GO

The best time to visit a campus is when school is in session. Summer visits, as convenient as they may be to schedule, won't give you or your child the real flavor of what the college experience is like. For the same reason, weekday visits are preferable to weekend ones.

Be sure to let the school know you're coming. You don't appreciate people just dropping in on you, do you? Besides, they'll help you make the most of the trip.

Secret #62

You Never Know Who You're **Talking** To

Parents have become so overbearing during campus visits that a number of schools have introduced student-only tours. That means parents are corralled into their own tour or—even more dangerous—go wandering about unattended.

In either case, exploring the campus minus your offspring is no license to say whatever pops into your head. Why? Because you never know exactly who it is you're speaking with. That approachable-looking young fellow could turn out to be your kid's resident advisor, or a graduate teaching assistant. Who knows, he could even be your kid's first philosophy professor (and you know how *they* blab). You don't want anything you say or do coming back to haunt your freshman.

Some questions you probably don't want to ask:

* Can my kid take cell calls in class if they're from his mother?
* Can my child bring a hypoallergenic mattress?
* What genius thought up coed bathrooms?

- Where do the really smart kids hang out?
- Where do the really rich kids hang out?
- Do the Dead ever play here? I'm a real Deadhead!
- Why don't you have more Parents' Weekends?

In addition to keeping your questions objective, have a care about sharing those when-I-was-in-college stories. Assume anyone can tell just by looking at you now that you were cool, if a bit wild and crazy, back then. The really cool people never need to make a point of it, now, do they?

If you obey the preceding rules, you can reunite with your child after your respective tours with your head held high. Now, when you do show up for Parents' Weekend, they won't have to resort to the I-never-saw-those-people-before-in-my-life strategy. Who knows? You might even get a hug.

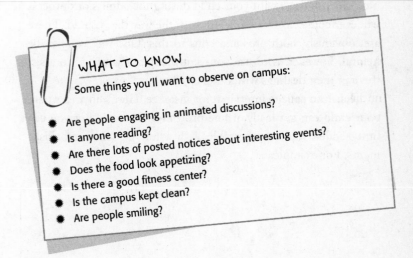

WHAT TO KNOW

Some things you'll want to observe on campus:

- Are people engaging in animated discussions?
- Is anyone reading?
- Are there lots of posted notices about interesting events?
- Does the food look appetizing?
- Is there a good fitness center?
- Is the campus kept clean?
- Are people smiling?

Secret #63

Some Things Only a Parent Can Say

No one who deals with your child during the admissions process will ever come close to knowing them the way that you do. There are, obviously, both pros and cons to this. One way you can be helpful, however, is to use your knowledge of your kid to assist them in their dealings with others.

Take the college interview, for instance. Here's an area where your child can get loads of fine professional advice. But you can bring added value to the table with a few personal embellishments. For example:

Standard Advice	Added Parental Value Advice
Smile.	First make sure there's nothing in your teeth.
Make eye contact.	Don't stare, or you'll look like Hannibal Lecter.
Shake hands firmly.	Trim those fingernails.
Dress casually but neatly.	Burn your wardrobe; start over.
Speak up.	Pipe down. The interviewer wants a chance to talk, too.
Ask questions.	But not ones you should already know the answers to.
Be yourself.	Be your best self. Because you know that self that gets all whiny and sulky and speaks in monosyllables? Well, that one can be really annoying.
Don't overstay your welcome.	Don't stand around hemming and hawing. Get out of there and call us!

Secret #64

Silence Is **Golden,** Sometimes Platinum

There's a useful rule of thumb when it comes to answering questions in stressful situations. It's a four-letter word and easy to remember, though not so easy to do. The word is s-t-o-p.

As communication experts—and trial lawyers—attest, the first thing that comes out of our mouths in high-stress situations is rarely the thing that best conveys our point of view. When we leave a job interview or step down from a witness stand or conclude a friendly chat with an IRS auditor, we are likely to dwell on all the shoulda-woulda-coulda answers that eluded us in the moment. The same, alas, too often applies to the college interview: Why didn't I tell that guy about my interest in international relations? Why didn't I mention my mentoring experience? Why did I say I really liked the dorms instead of, "I want a strong core curriculum"?

We live in a culture addicted to speed. We believe that "dead air" is undesirable and that silence is awkward. We don't want to look like we don't know what to say, so we tend to say whatever first pops into our heads. If only we'd counted to three inside those heads before we gushed out a reply.

It may be hard for you to believe that the same child who has answered your "How was school today?" queries with a half-hearted grunt since puberty would be prone to blather on to a college interviewer, but trust me, they will, *because the stakes are so high.*

If you really want to help your kid with their interview, encourage them to practice silent reflection with a friend who's also about to undergo the college-interview process. It feels odd at first, and although those three seconds feel like an eternity to the person answering questions, the time lapse will not make the interviewer uncomfortable.

During those precious few seconds, the "askee" might discover that *they didn't really hear the question.* That's another common interview stumbling block. When stress is high, we are so busy anticipating what we think the interviewer will ask us, that we don't know what they *actually* did ask. It's perfectly fine to paraphrase a question and repeat it back to the interviewer to determine exactly what they want to know.

Taking a few moments to think over an answer doesn't make one look dense; it makes one seem thoughtful. Making sure you are answering the right question shows a regard for accurate self-representation.

Secret #65

Body Language Says a Lot

People communicate on conscious and unconscious levels. College interviewers, being people, are as likely to be influenced on the latter level as anyone else. There are a few simple strategies you might want to impart to your child that will provide them with a slight subliminal benefit.

The first one involves what's known as "mirroring posture." When two individuals are getting along well, they adopt what researchers call *postural congruence* or *postural echoes*. This means they unconsciously adopt the same ways of holding and arranging their bodies. Mirror-image postural echoes—when one person's left side reflects the other person's right side—are the strongest indication of rapport between any two people.

Experimenters have shown that although people are not consciously aware of someone deliberately mirroring their postures, they will nevertheless evaluate a person who does so very favorably. To foster a sense of harmony and like-mindedness with someone, any of us can consciously arrange our body and limbs to mirror theirs (e.g., leaning forward with your right arm on the table when they are leaning forward with their left arm on the table).

Communication researchers have also found that nodding can be used to enhance conversations. Making single, brief nods while someone is speaking acts as a sign of attentiveness and approval—and keeps the speaker speaking. This comes in handy if the interviewee wants the interviewer to spend more time talking, the upshot being, of course, that *they* will have to do less. You might think that's counterproductive in an interview, but people usually report a positive reaction to a conversation in which they were allowed to do most of the talking. (Double nods, by the way, change the rate at which the other person speaks, usually speeding up the flow. This comes in handy for someone who just wants the interview to be finished—though I don't necessarily recommend it.)

Is all of this unconscious stuff a kind of cheating? No, no, no. These are things that we tend to do naturally and intuitively—except when we are very nervous, in which case we may freeze up and appear stiff and wooden. Becoming aware of our natural tendencies and reinstating them just makes conversation flow more smoothly and makes situations like interviews more pleasant for everyone involved.

Nod like you agree.

Secret #66

Some Things **Are** Skin Deep

During the middle-school years, preadolescents are more preoccupied with their physical appearance than with any other aspect of themselves. Once they're in high school, however, studies show they are primarily concerned with academic performance.

I suppose there are two ways to view this phenomenon. One is that developing teens are becoming less shallow. The other is that they're becoming increasingly unkempt.

In truth, a certain amount of adolescent energy *should* rightfully be allocated to obsessive hair combing, skin exfoliation, and clothes shopping. Yes, perhaps even some of the energy that they now spend practicing quadratic equations and boning up on the periodic table of elements.

Good grooming and a pleasing appearance contribute to college-interview success—just as they do to job-interview success. A review of experimental studies clearly shows that physical attractiveness for both men and women is of considerable significance in the occupational realm. Overwhelmingly, attractive people fare better in terms of perceived job qualifications, hiring recommendations, and predicted job success.

I know, I know. Beneath every frog may lie the heart of a prince. But frogs rarely make it into management training.

No one is suggesting that prepping for a college interview means pulling your child off the debate team to make time for hair highlighting and microdermabrasion. But if your overly studious student is falling prey to sleepless nights and a French-fries-on-the-run diet, remind them to consider whether the dark undereye-circle look suits them.

Take a breather from SAT prep once in a while and bring them to your gym or to a day spa. Before the interview itself, spring for a good haircut and a few classic wardrobe pieces. There's nothing wrong, albeit in moderation, with some good old-fashioned looks obsession. Ask any frog.

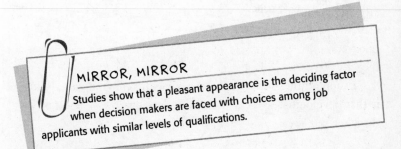

MIRROR, MIRROR

Studies show that a pleasant appearance is the deciding factor when decision makers are faced with choices among job applicants with similar levels of qualifications.

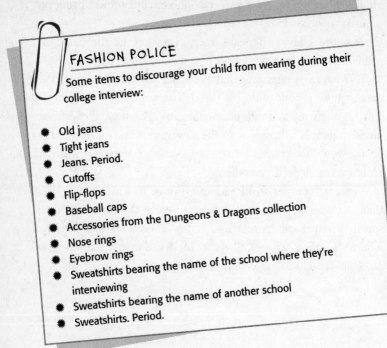

FASHION POLICE

Some items to discourage your child from wearing during their college interview:

* Old jeans
* Tight jeans
* Jeans. Period.
* Cutoffs
* Flip-flops
* Baseball caps
* Accessories from the Dungeons & Dragons collection
* Nose rings
* Eyebrow rings
* Sweatshirts bearing the name of the school where they're interviewing
* Sweatshirts bearing the name of another school
* Sweatshirts. Period.

Chapter 10: It's an **Investment,** Right?

The **Financials**

Secret #67

Classroom Customers **Care**

Want to make certain you have enough money to cover the entire cost of your child's college education? Go back in your time machine and invest a couple of thousand dollars. Buy dot-coms and sell them before they crash. Buy MCI and Enron and sell them before anybody goes to jail. Now, take all your profits and buy treasury bills that come due in a laddered fashion, one for each of your child's four college years.

What? Time machine broken? Yeah, mine, too. There's just no quality control on those things.

Okay, try this: Contribute what you can and have your child take out loans, participate in work-study, get a part-time job, or sell some stuff on eBay. If you feel guilty about saddling them with financial responsibility, consider the upsides of that responsibility.

As a college teacher myself, I often notice a difference in attitude between students whose parents are footing all the bills and those who are paying at least some expenses themselves. Those who pay can be much more focused and determined. They often work harder, read more, and tackle the extra-credit assignments. They ask more of their instructors, too. They stay after class to prolong discussions of topics that interest them. They ask what they can do to gain a deeper understanding. They feel—and they should—like they deserve to get their money's worth. They ask the best of themselves, their teachers, and the school administration.

Even if you can afford to pay for all your child's college expenses, you might consider asking them to participate by paying for books, some student fees, cell phone bills, clothing and entertainment expenses, and the like. To appropriate an old-fashioned notion, self-reliance builds character. They can't sign up for a course in that (but if they could, they ought to pay for it).

MORE STUDENTS RECEIVE AID

Student financial aid in 2002–2003 rose to a record level of more than $105 billion. A majority of students receive some form of aid, though less of it now comes in the form of grants than previously. Most aid is awarded through low-interest loans.

Loans comprise 54 percent of the aid awarded each year. Most students can expect to receive a loan as part of a financial-aid package.

Secret #68

Work-Study Reaps **Rewards**

How about this for a tuition payment you might like? Zero. Yes, zero. The College of the Ozarks, a small Missouri school, charges no tuition whatsoever. Students pay their way by working at a number of jobs ranging from working in the campus restaurant and bakery to the college-run construction company, the fire department, the machine shop, the water-treatment plant, and even the farm. Their duties might include pounding nails, milking cows, making apple butter, and baking cakes.

The College of the Ozarks was founded nearly a century ago. For its first fifty years, it was a boarding school for disadvantaged elementary and high school students. It taught them vocational skills while requiring them to pay their way through. In the mid-1960s, the school became a college and retained the ethic of emphasizing character and work. In fact, signs peppering the campus proudly proclaim the college's nickname: Hard Work U.

Of course, the thing about hard work is that it's . . . well, hard. Students often have to leave for their jobs by 5 A.M. They have to learn how to juggle the responsibilities of their jobs with the rest of their demanding schedules. Sound familiar? To me, it sounds exactly like real life. What could constitute better preparation?

Think it's worth a shot? Okay, but this is no sure bet. The College of the Ozarks now receives a dozen applications for every opening. The school's low acceptance rate ranks it just under Juilliard, Harvard, Princeton, and Columbia. What we need are more schools like this one. But for now, if your kid can't attend this one, look at work-study options that merit partial tuition at other schools. And remember the Ozarks philosophy: Hard work provides self-confidence rooted in genuine accomplishment. Sweat equity pays.

It puts the prospect of your child working part-time at the campus bookstore in a whole new light, doesn't it?

WINNING THROUGH HARD WORK

Research shows that students who work a moderate amount often do better academically. Securing an on-campus job is a good way to help cover college costs, gain experience, and foster ties with the school community.

Secret #69

Kindness **Pays**

A plethora of niche scholarships is available for students with characteristics, penchants, and predilections that mesh with those held dear by the scholarships' endowers. There are special scholarships for tall people, short people, sets of twins, left-handed people, and people born with the surname "Zolp." Skateboarders, duck callers, Tupperware dealers, and those with a really good recipe for apple pie may also merit scholarship funds. Likewise for students studying parapsychology, grapes and wine-making, mycology (that would be spores, mold, and fungus), and aquatic entomology (that would be freshwater insects). If your kid will agree to write an essay on *The Fountainhead* or show up at their prom in an outfit made of duct tape, there might be big scholarship bucks in the offing.

But here's my favorite: At Hiram College in Ohio, the Hal Reicle Memorial Scholarship is given to students based on their anonymous acts of kindness. This scholarship was endowed by family and friends of a Hiram graduate who died in the Persian

Gulf War and who was known for the great pleasure he took in helping others—often in secret. Recipients are chosen on the basis of their humanitarian efforts, community involvement, and volunteerism. The prize committee relies solely on what it calls its army of stealthy observers, the Secret Society of Serendipitous Service to Hal (SSSSH!). The group's mission is to identify students of strong moral character with a spirit of giving and dedication to others.

So, no, you can't get an application or nominate your child. But you can remind them that while the tendency of people in high-pressure, competitive circumstances is to become exclusively self-involved, a little selflessness provides a nice, calming change in perspective and—who knows—might result in some surprise college dollars. Encourage your kid to help out a stranger today. You never know when SSSSH! will be lurking.

FYI

According to Sallie Mae, the corporation created by Congress to provide financial aid and information, college scholarships based on almost every imaginable qualification add up to more than 2.4 million awards worth more than $14 billion each year.

SOME MORE INTERESTING SCHOLARSHIPS

* The CIA gives financial assistance to students pursuing a number of majors, including geography and international studies.
* The Klingon Language Institute awards the Kor Memorial Scholarship to reward achievements in language study (no Klingon required).
* SPAACSE (the Society of Performers, Artists, Athletes, and Celebrities for Space Exploration) offers awards to students pursuing an interest in "space music" or "space art" that celebrates the beauty of the universe.
* Descendants of the Signers of the Declaration of Independence gives scholarships to, you guessed it, descendants of the signers of the Declaration of Independence.

Secret #70

Consider the "C" Words

Brace yourself, because we're going to talk about *the C words*—the words that often strike fear in the heart of any parent of an aspiring university student: community college. For years, you may have been using the very idea of a two-year community college as a prod with which to motivate a slacking high schooler: "If you don't get cracking on that trigonometry, buddy, you'll end up in . . . community college." Probably community college scared you more than it did your daydreaming offspring; nevertheless, its lack of brand name cachet was often enough to generate at least a cursory stab at math homework.

But if you think of community college as a worst-case scenario—useful only for frightening fifteen-year-olds into submission—think again. Many people now have a higher regard for community colleges than they ever have had before. What do they know that you may not?

For one thing, they may know kids who actually *went* to community college. These may have been kids who didn't quite know what they wished to focus their studies on and wanted some time to explore options while still earning college credits. They may have been kids whose high school grades were less than stellar and who wanted a second chance to boost their academic record. They may have been kids who needed to save some money, which they certainly did.

What happens to students after community college? In increasing numbers, they're transferring their credits to four-year institutions. They're tens of thousands of dollars ahead of the game and surer of their goals than they could have been at age eighteen. *Ah, but are they prepared?* Well, they've probably been in smaller classes than they would have been if they'd attended large universities, and they probably had more contact with their instructors (many of whom probably also teach at nearby four-year schools).

It's true that two-year community colleges are not residential, so graduates haven't yet been afforded many cultural advantages available to their four-year peers. They're woefully behind in coed bathroom etiquette and will require training as to which dining-hall entrees will cause instant, as opposed to gradual, coronary disease. They've most likely been to fewer frat parties and may have fewer sources for obtaining fake IDs. But, hey, they've still got two years to catch up, and I, for one, have faith in the resilience of youth. So should you.

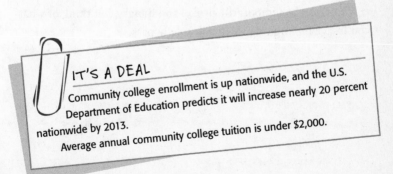

IT'S A DEAL

Community college enrollment is up nationwide, and the U.S. Department of Education predicts it will increase nearly 20 percent nationwide by 2013.

Average annual community college tuition is under $2,000.

Secret #71

College Costs Are **Relative**

Got your first tuition bill in hand? Think about this: Americans spend more on fast food each year than they do on higher education. Makes sense. College only lasts four years (okay, sometimes five or six), but we can wear our Whoppers on our hips forever.

Of course, since *your* family will be spending so much more on the higher education than many of your fellow citizens, you will be compensating for everyone else who is up to their double chins in special sauce and onion rings.

You may be temporarily broke, and hungry, but think of what you'll save by forgoing the quadruple bypass.

Flash Card

It's All About Vocabulary—the "T" Words

Tangential—Facts that are beside the point, for example, any award your child won in kindergarten.

Trifling—See above.

Trite—Shallow, superficial statements, such as those to be avoided on essays (e.g., "World peace would be good.").

Tome—Something an admissions officer does not want or need to read.

Truncate—Something your kid should do to their application tome.

Trepidation—Fear, dread, anxiety. Supply your own synonym here:

_____

_____

_____

_____

_____

_____

Chapter 11: And the **Envelope,** Please . . .

Secret #72

Whose **Mail** Is It, Anyway?

Who should open the letters that arrive from colleges? Your kid should.

But what if the envelope is fat?

They should.

But what if the envelope is thin?

They should.

But what if . . .

They should.

I know you're dying to know if they got in. And you will know soon enough. But if you open the letters, you put yourself in the position of either (a) being the bearer of bad news, at which point you may have to remind them not to shoot the messenger, or (b) being the bearer of good news, which they would have relished more if you hadn't intervened in their moment of triumph.

Don't worry. Soon you will have lots and lots of mail from your kid's college-to-be, and you'll have lots of opportunities to reply. You can develop the same warm, friendly correspondence with the folks in the bursar's office that you have with your mortgage lender and the electric company.

In the meanwhile, when that long-awaited piece of mail comes addressed to your child, call and let them know that they've got a missive waiting. Then put the letter under a vase or a magazine and distract yourself. Watch *Oprah* or something. No, no, don't hold it up to the light. Put it back, I tell you. Really, don't. Oh, well, okay—just a little peek then. But don't *open* the thing. That's the really important part.

WHO GOES ONLINE?

If your child has applied to a school that allows them to access admissions outcomes online, the same principle applies. Who gets to go online first? They do.

Secret #73

Acceptance Takes **Time** to Accept

It's the big day, and, lo and behold, the envelope is fat. They're in. And it's the school they really, really, really wanted to go to.

Are they happy? Yes! And no!

Why the mixed emotions? Come on, you've been there, too. You know that getting what you want can be daunting. Were you really supposed to get it? Was there some mistake? Are you really just a fraud? That's some of what your kid is going through.

Psychologists often write about the "fear of success." It's a natural phenomenon. Your newly official college student is certainly susceptible. Part of them may worry that once they arrive on campus, everyone will figure out that they're a lucky pretender. Surely there's some truly worthy kid out there whose slot they were given, and that kid's weeping over their thin envelope right now.

Another noted accompaniment to achieving a much-strived-for goal is a sense of loneliness. Suddenly the future is real, and we're headed toward it—all by ourselves. This is never more applicable than when one is heading off to the great unknown of college life, leaving everything and everyone familiar behind.

Then there's the knee-jerk second-guessing impulse. Is what they thought they wanted in fact what they really wanted? Maybe they should have spent more time thinking it over? Is it too late to change their mind?

Any and all of these are normal reactions. Understand that your child may experience them and try to be sensitive. Yes, congratulations are in order. But give your kid time to process what's happened before you start shouting in the street within earshot of the neighbors and calling near and distant relations to spread the word. There's plenty of time to celebrate. Allow a little time to ponder. Once your child identifies their fears, they'll figure out how to handle success—and so will you.

IF THEIR CUP RUNNETH OVER

Being accepted by more than one desired school can be quite a heady sensation—for a bit. Then it sinks in, *they* have to choose. Suggest a spreadsheet, with all the pros and cons. Factor in the financials. If it's at all feasible, plan repeat visits to the schools that said yes. But in the end, they'll have to go with their gut. They'll have to trust their instincts, and you'll have to respect those instincts.

Secret #74

Whatever Happens, Celebrate

Many have described the college-admissions process as an adolescent rite of passage akin to tribal rituals in which youngsters undergo a challenging ordeal, the completion of which allows them to take their place in the adult community. In certain ways, the analogy holds. But one important element is missing: the celebration. Every good rite of passage should culminate with feasting, music, and merriment.

Plan a bash for when your child is accepted at college.

In fact, start thinking about your celebrations during the grueling admissions process to lighten your mood. One of the things that got me through childbirth labor was to keep reminding myself, "A year from now, you'll be at a birthday party."

Acceptances aren't the only thing you can celebrate. A growing trend is to host "rejection" parties, where the price of admission is to bring at least one rejection letter.

Secret #75

On the Wait List? Eat a Strawberry

A Zen parable tells of a man being chased by a bloodthirsty tiger. The tiger pursues him to the edge of a cliff where, unable to think of any other option, he jumps off the edge. Partway down, he's able to grasp on to a dangling vine, which will soon snap under his weight. The tiger waits above; an abyss looms below. While the man dangles from the vine, he spies a berry growing there and plucks and eats the fruit.

Remember this parable should your child be one of the many college applicants who, when the first round is over, is neither accepted nor rejected but put on hold.

One-third of all colleges—and over three-fourths of selective ones—maintain wait lists, and list size is growing proportional to marketplace competition. More students are applying to more schools, and schools need a backup plan to make certain they fill their freshman classes with qualified candidates. Good for them; bad for you and your family if you're not the sort of people who thrive on uncertainty.

Who is? Well, Zen guy, for one. Suspended in a moment of what can only be considered supreme cosmic ambiguity, he makes the most of the moment he's been given.

But what would that involve for a wait-listed candidate?

Most admissions officers say there's little you can do to change your wait-list status. Only a mere fraction of those left dangling on the list will get in, and that is largely determined by demographic factors. (To help round out a freshman class geographically, you could consider relocating your teenager to, say, Wyoming.)

The best way to allay wait-list anxiety is to focus positively and productively on the time you have together before things change next September. Teach your kids how to do a load of wash for those times when they run out of underwear and simply can't make it home for the weekend; show them how to balance a checkbook. Join them in a calming pastime that doesn't count as "achievement" (hiking, biking, watching game shows). When in doubt, savor a strawberry. Or make it a pizza. It's the savoring that counts.

WAITING IT OUT

About a third of colleges use wait lists, according to the National Association for College Admission Counseling. Colleges that admit fewer than half of their applicants use wait lists at a much higher rate than those that admit more than half. In other words, the more selective the school, the higher the chances of being wait-listed.

Although the number of colleges using wait lists has remained steady for many years, the number of students placed on wait lists has increased. On average, 12 percent of students who apply to institutions that have a wait list are placed on the list. As a national average, a student's chance of being accepted from a wait list is one in five.

Secret #76

Sometimes Doing **Nothing** Is Something

Is your child still on that wait list? Are you all getting antsy despite your vow to chill? You're undoubtedly going to come across a good deal of advice that urges applicants in limbo to remain proactive under such circumstances. It can feel like welcome advice, because it caters to your urge to *do something*. But have a care: This is a bit of counsel to be taken only moderately to heart.

An applicant who lets a school know they'll attend if accepted may indeed gain a slight advantage. Schools hate rejection as much as applicants do, and they are glad to know of a sure thing. But regaling an admissions officer with a continued barrage of eleventh-hour achievements won't help an applicant unless the alleged achievements really are achievements, and not mere afterthoughts.

Did your son or daughter just win a Pulitzer Prize or a Tony Award? That's worth an express-mail letter. Did they just self-publish a pamphlet of haiku or win a featured role in the drama club's *Pirates of Penzance*? I know you're proud, but save the postage. As paradoxical as it may seem, and as much as you may resist believing it, there are times when doing nothing *is* doing something. As for how many après-wait-list communiqués they should send to admissions officers overall, let them be guided by this simple principle: Nobody likes a stalker, and few will invite them to come and live closer.

Secret #77

You Can't Take It **Personally**

There are certain things in life that you just can't take personally. These include:

* rain
* traffic
* the New York Mets
* buying a losing lottery ticket
* being rejected by your dream school

Rejection by a school is rejection of an application, not a person. Countless random factors play a role in deciding which applications make the yes pile and which do not. Universities of national standing want students from all over the country. State colleges want students from all over the state. Some schools like legacies; some like applicants who will be first-generation college attendees. Sometimes an application will land on exactly the right person's desk at exactly the right moment; sometimes an application will land on exactly the wrong person's desk at the wrong moment. That, of course, is the most random factor of all.

Everyone knows someone at the top of their class, with killer SAT scores and enough community service to make Mother Teresa blush, who *still* didn't get into their first-choice school. Such horror stories are not apocryphal, they are real. But here is a story that, in its way, is even more disturbing: I know a young man who strived for years so that he could get into his dream school, which happened to be Notre Dame. On paper he looked like an ideal match, but, alas, he was wait-listed. While he was preparing, rather sulkily, to go to his second-choice school, he received Notre Dame's belated letter of acceptance. Did he go? No. Notre Dame, he said, had hurt his feelings.

His feelings may well have been hurt, of course, but no one at Notre Dame set out to make this earnest young man unhappy by wait-listing him. Nor for that matter did anyone set out to make him happy by accepting him. The simple truth is that he first failed to clear, but ultimately did clear, some unknown demographic hurdle. Luck, or lack thereof, was a major factor in both events.

Lots of emotions get stirred up during the admissions process. In addition to moments of triumph and relief, there will almost certainly be moments of dejection and outrage. Let's remember to tell our children: We can't control events, but we can control our responses to them. Not every feeling should be acted upon. And not everything that happens should be taken personally. While we're at it, let's try to remember this ourselves. I know I'll try to the next time I'm stuck in traffic on a rainy night—a night when the New York Mets lose again.

Secret #78

Good Learners Learn **Anywhere**

If your child does not get into their most desired college—or the college you most wanted them to attend—their opportunities for learning have not been curtailed. Good learners learn anywhere. That is one thing we all should have learned by now.

Oh, and another thing we should have learned: good teachers teach everywhere. So do so-so ones. A student can be bored to tears—no, make that wracking sobs—in a hallowed Ivy League lecture hall. Another student can be enthralled by an ingenious professor they stumble upon at a community college when all the courses they really wanted to take were closed.

And, of course, learning need not be limited to academic environs. More now than ever, the knowledge base of humankind is available for access. Anything one wishes to know can be known. Is there anything wrong with being an autodidact? Certainly not. Remember, the self-taught always have the advantage of truly admiring their teachers.

Secret #79

Rejection Has Upsides

Look at it this way: If your child had gotten into every school they'd applied to, you'd then have to watch them agonize, once again, over what to do. Sometimes having a decision made for you is not the worst thing in the world.

Besides, if they'd been accepted everywhere, you would have always worried that they'd set their sights too low, now, wouldn't you?

Secret #80

Why Ask **Why?**

If a school declines to admit your child, the temptation may be to ask for an explanation. What, exactly, was the problem? Was it your child's choice of essay topic? Was it their array of extracurricular activities? Was it that sophomore B-minus in French *(mon Dieu!)*?

Chances are it was none of the above. Many schools are able to fill their freshman classes twice over with qualified applicants. Your child may well have been eminently qualified and still not have gotten in.

Your thirst for such enlightenment is understandable. After all that you and your kid have been through, a vague and summary rejection seems downright heartless. Well, how shall I phrase this . . . get over it. Studies show that even applicants who feel devastated by rejection from a school recover their emotional equilibrium within about two weeks. I haven't seen any studies on their parents, but I'm guessing the same applies.

Secret #81
Appeals Are Not So Appealing

Some schools have a process for appealing a rejection. Some provide opportunities for submitting new academic information, such as updated grades. Does this mean you should encourage your child to put themselves through this process? Only if you, and they, are truly gluttons for punishment.

Most applicants do not win an appeal. If they do, they may only get the right to request a spot on the wait list. (More uncertainty!) Appeals are worth the effort for people who've wrongfully been sentenced to life imprisonment. In this case, they're a time-consuming emotional drain. Don't go there. Help your child consider the choices that are available to them and choose the best one. That's the really appealing thing to do.

Secret #82

Remember Hamilton's Revenge

Alexander Hamilton, although not well-born like most of America's founding fathers, was well known by the age of seventeen for his remarkable abilities as a writer and visionary. Alas, he was not so highly regarded by Princeton University, which declined to admit him as a freshman when he applied. He instead went to King's College, now Columbia University.

The result: Instead of being relegated to what were, in those days, the boondocks of New Jersey, Hamilton found himself smack in the heart of New York's intensely stimulating intellectual and political milieu and thriving commercial economy. In this city, as *American Heritage* put it, "his commercial instincts could flourish most abundantly." Later, as America's first secretary of the treasury, Hamilton "made the American economy not just an engine of wealth but an engine of economic opportunity."

He also ended up on the $10 bill.

Princeton, take that.

AND IN A MORE RECENT REJECTION EPISODE . . .

When renowned psychologist and author Martin Seligman was rejected from Harvard, he assumed he was "a failure in life, not really 'good enough.' " Nursing his wounds, he went to Princeton, where he graduated summa cum laude.

Subsequently, Seligman devoted much of his prominent career to studying resilience, optimism, and positive thinking. He wrote numerous bestsellers on these topics and founded the Institute for Positive Psychology at the University of Pennsylvania.

Seligman has said he knew he had fully recovered from the indignity of Harvard's snub the first time they offered him a job—and he turned them down.

Secret #83

Luck Is Dumb; Your Kid Is **Not**

So, your kid was rejected. Was it *your* fault?

Yes.

They would have had a better shot if only you'd gotten on this college thing right away. If only you had hummed Mozart throughout their gestation, breast-fed them until their first T-ball game, and awakened them every four hours for cribside flash-card drills.

Just kidding.

Demographic realities being what they are, rejection from a school often does not signify anything more than that too many other kids who were somewhat like your kid tried to get in. That doesn't mean that your kid is dumb or that you are. The deciding factor may well have been luck. They don't call it "dumb luck" for nothing.

What if your kid is berating himself for not getting in? Be empathic, be a comfort, but also be clear: It's honorable to take personal accountability where appropriate, but it's hubris to hold oneself accountable for the outcome of events over which one had no ultimate control. That's one of the things that you, as an adult, know for sure. Isn't it?

Okay, just checking. Now, go ahead and commiserate. You all need a hug.

TEN WAYS TO COMFORT YOUR DISAPPOINTED KID

1. Provide lotion-infused tissues for a good cry.
2. TiVo their favorite funny shows for when they're ready to laugh again.
3. Cook the warm, gooey foods they loved when they were five.
4. Dig out their old teddy bear.
5. Give them permission to pound a pillow.
6. Let them sleep in and sulk for a day if they need to.
7. Encourage them to talk with friends in similar circumstances.
8. Apply serious shopping therapy.
9. Read them Secret #82.
10. Remind them that one of the laws of the universe is that the finest people, most brilliant ideas, and worthiest book manuscripts always suffer initial rejection.

Secret #84

Don't Rain on Anyone's Parade

What should your kid do if one of their classmates got a college acceptance that makes them green with envy? What if they got in somewhere that they both applied to—and your child did not get accepted? They should do the same thing you should do—have all the feelings they need to have, but don't rain on anyone else's parade.

Smile. Say congratulations. Clap them on the back (not *too* hard now).

Then, silently to yourselves, remember what a sagacious holy man in Kathmandu said about all the commotion surrounding the summiting of Mount Everest: "Why all the excitement? Isn't it just another place?"

Secret #85

Take a **Quantum Leap**

Not entirely pleased with your child's acceptances? Think about this: For a long time now, quantum physicists have postulated the existence of parallel universes in which every possible outcome of a situation can unfold. If this theory holds, there may well be a universe somewhere in which your child gained admission to MIT. Best of all, they're sending the parallel parents the tuition bill.

Secret #86

Be **Happy** for Them

No matter where your child ends up going to school, be enthusiastic. Enthusiasm—like the flu—is massively contagious. If you're excited, chances are they will be, too. They'll head off with a better attitude about themselves and about their future classmates, and they'll fit into their new community all the better for it.

Joining that community with a positive attitude is important. Making the most of that during college—participating in school events, joining organizations, attending extracurricular lectures and discussions—will provide much-needed emotional sustenance. It can also help pave the way toward a successful future, because after graduation, chums become alums who can continue to network, share information and contacts, and help one another in the workplace and in all aspects of life.

SOMETIMES IT'S WHO YOU KNOW

Alumni connections are one of the best ways of finding employment. People like to hire others with whom they have had a shared experience and with whom they share loyalties.

Secret #87

It's **Never** Too Late

When anxiety seems overwhelming, it can be calming to envision a worst-case-scenario outcome and then imagine how you will deal with it. So, hypothetically, what if the thing you fear most happens? What if your worst nightmare materializes and all your child's envelopes come back thin? Does unilateral rejection mean a life of lawn mowing and lifeguarding?

Nah.

Applicants who don't get in to the first batch of schools to which they applied can access a wide-ranging survey of space availability from the "late-admissions list," made available from the National Association for College Admission Counseling. They can also check with any individual school that has a rolling-admissions policy. Since rolling-admissions schools accept applications throughout the year, they will certainly consider late enrollees if their freshman class is not filled. Students should also consult with their school counselor, who may well have the skinny on freshman slots still available.

There are far more good opportunities for late admissions than you might imagine. These often include state universities (sometimes not the main campus, but one that is a fine starting place with transfer potential) and small liberal arts colleges. Look especially to areas of the country where the eighteen-year-old population is on the decline rather than on the increase.

If your high schooler applied to a balanced mix of schools with realistic good-fit and safety options, they are not likely to need a Plan B. But it doesn't hurt to know there is one.

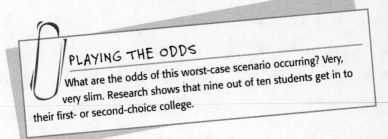

PLAYING THE ODDS

What are the odds of this worst-case scenario occurring? Very, very slim. Research shows that nine out of ten students get in to their first- or second-choice college.

LATE ADMISSIONS OPPORTUNITIES

As of late June 2005, the website of the National Association of College Admissions Counselors listed more than 250 colleges and universities that still had openings for qualified applicants. Among them:

Smith College

Notre Dame

University of Arizona

University of San Diego

California College of the Arts

University of Colorado, Denver

University of Iowa

University of Maine

University of Massachusetts, Lowell

University of Massachusetts, Dartmouth

Saint Louis University

Drew University (New Jersey)

Fordham University (New York)

Hofstra University (New York)

State University of New York, Brockport

State University of New York, Oswego

University of Dallas

University of Oregon

Secret #88

They **Did** It . . . You Helped

When all's said and done, remember whose achievement getting into college was. Your child's.

They got through biology and trigonometry and world history. They learned to write a thesis essay. They slogged through the SATs. They took on the activities—the band, the tennis team, the volunteer work. They bonded with teachers who thought enough of them to write letters of recommendation for them. They sweated out the months of uncertainty.

Were you by their side? Yes. Did you do your job? Admirably. But the bulk of the kudos is theirs—and the adventure on which they are embarking is theirs to make of what they will.

You should be proud of yourself, no question, but you should be even more proud of them. Because that's what being a parent means.

I know you know. This is just a gentle reminder.

Flash Card

It's All About Vocabulary—the "Q" Words

Quixotic—Overly idealistic and impractical, as in applying only to "reach" schools and ignoring the safety zone.

Quotidian—Occurring daily, commonplace, as in the number of applicants who take a quixotic approach.

Quittance—A document that releases one from debt or obligation, such as the kind you hope to get from the Financial Aid Office (see *quixotic*, above).

Querulous—Fault-finding, whiny, and complaining in tone, such as how you sound when you ask your kid if they've actually studied any of their vocabulary words.

Quizzical—The look you get in response to your querulous query.

Quaff—To drink in large gulps, with great relish. Cocktails, anyone?

Chapter 12: There They Go . . .

for Now

Secret #89

Senioritis Happens

Think of it as the Big Loaf. They've been accepted to college, but they don't have to do any college work yet. They've gotten far enough into senior year that they know they're likely to pass all their courses unless they pepper their teachers with extreme spitballs. And they won't do that because, frankly, it would take too much effort.

Right now it's all about lethargy. Once upon a time, they thought that was just an SAT word, but now they realize it's a lifestyle. In the months between gaining admission to college and officially embarking on the next part of their life, your soon-to-be undergrad will shift out of high gear and transform into the Little Engine That Couldn't. They will resist household rules, social conventions, and—in the case of certain young men—personal hygiene niceties. You may not see much of them, but you'll know where they've been; like garden slugs, they will leave behind a telltale trail of slime. Respect? As the late Rodney Dangerfield would have put it: You won't get none. At least, not so you'd notice. But don't worry. It's all unfolding the way it's supposed to. Senioritis serves an evolutionary purpose.

Remember back when they first morphed from sweet, innocent children into sullen, surly teens? You wondered where your little baby had gone, and that was the point. They'd been programmed to repel you so that you could tolerate—even welcome—a growing sense of separateness from them. By the time their hormones calmed a bit, you'd gotten out of anachronistic habits like snuggling with them in bed each night and picking out their clothes. You had, mostly without words, renegotiated the boundaries that governed your relationship. During the summer before college, this will happen yet again. By the time they pack up and go, you're supposed to be eager to hand them their hat—if you can locate their hat amidst the rubble.

Chances are your formal parting may even conclude on a somewhat sour note. You'll drive them to campus and, inevitably, do something to mortify them in front of their new roommate. You'll brand them as a misfit in front of all potential friends and romantic partners by virtue of what you wear or how you insist on carrying their boxes or how you pretend to be cool about the coed bathrooms. You'll notice, out of the corner of your teary eye, their apologetic eye-rolls meant to signify, "I only humor these people because they write my tuition checks."

Remain calm. Make a swift and gracious exit and put some miles between you and your little ingrate before you stop to imbibe some well-deserved refreshment. By the time you get home, or shortly thereafter, a flood of chatty cell calls and newsy e-mails will begin. Even if your child is not telling you about their new experiences in detail (a blessing), they'll want to touch base. Let them. Shoot the breeze with them, offer tidbits of news from the home front, send love from the pets. Your relationship boundaries, stretched so far, are on the move again. This time, they're inching in your direction. From your freshman's point of view, it's okay to be closer now that they're far away.

Secret #90

Think About a **Time-Out**

Remember time-out? When your little one got too worked up and frenzied, you had them take a break from their activity to chill and to ground themselves. Then they could continue without distress and avoid tantrums. Well, what if your kid wants a time-out now? What if—yes, after all of this—they want to consider deferring college for a year?

Don't dismiss it out of hand. Deferment has become entirely socially acceptable. Many college deans support it, saying it gives entering freshmen more focus and confidence. In fact—Anglophiles take note—in England, where young people do this routinely, time out between upper school and university has been given a very palatable name: the gap year.

No, no, this doesn't mean your kid will have to work at The Gap. A year deferred can be spent pursuing a passion, or, for those who are not sure what to study in college, discovering one. It can also simply be a much-needed break combining a program of study, travel, and work. (And, hey, if they happen to sell a few pairs of jeans and squirrel away a few dollars along the way, that wouldn't be so awful, would it?)

As the woeful mental health state of many college freshmen indicates, large numbers of kids are feeling burned out at high school's end. It makes sense that many would be better able to rededicate themselves to academic rigors once they've taken a breather. Imagine, if you can, having run a marathon, then being given a Mylar blanket and a medal, and then being escorted straight to the starting line of a triathlon. That's what going right into college feels like for a lot of graduating high school seniors, sometimes especially for achievers who went through high school full speed ahead.

Deferral is not for everyone, but if your child is tempted, it's worth some exploration. Time-outs were of value when your kid was little; they might still be of value now. Don't wait for a tantrum to erupt in order to find out.

HOLD YOUR HORSES?

In some instances, although they have not requested a deferral, college applicants are being sent a guaranteed acceptance by a school—for the year following the upcoming school year. If this happens to your kid, you, and they, might not want to reject this acceptance out of hand, particularly if the school is one they really want to attend. At least spend some time kicking around interesting ideas for the intervening year. And remember, things usually happen for a reason. . . .

Secret #91

College Education **Begins** at Home

Ten Things They Should Know Before They Go

1. Your honesty, or lack of it, on the roommate questionnaire has nothing to do with what kind of roommate you'll get. Be nice, anyway.

2. When you are closed out of a class you really want to take, try talking to the professor. You probably won't get in, but they may remember you next year when you do.

3. Never eat any dining-hall menu item that contains the words *surprise, mix,* or *fingers.*

4. Be especially polite to your roommate's parents. They might send you food.

5. Somehow, even in a wireless world, you can't have too many extension cords.

6. Lava lamps may be cool again, but you can't have mine.

7. The thing about credit card companies is they expect you to pay back the money. That's right, you, not me.

8. You can change your roommate next year—but change your sheets before then.

9. Oh, okay, you can have my lava lamp. But not my U2 poster.
10. A ninety-four-year-old West Virginia woman holds the record as the world's oldest person to graduate college. Don't break it.

PACK A COMFORT OBJECT

Among the essential things you should remind your freshman to pack for college are shower shoes and two alarm clocks (the second one set to go off after they ignore the first). I also suggest sneaking in their favorite stuffed animal.

You know the one: It's been chewed up and drooled on since babyhood. It's been carted on family trips and rescued from hotel laundry services while your little traveler sobbed for its return. It's been surreptitiously spirited off to summer camp and slumber parties, stuffed into the side zipper compartment of a duffel, but nonetheless kept close enough to offer comfort—because comfort is what it's all about.

Think no other freshmen will have them? Think again. The dorms of America are loaded with polka-dot hippos, ragged one-eared bunnies, and tattered coverlets.

Secret #92
Less Stress Now, Less Stress Later

America's college freshmen are showing up at school more stressed and anxious than ever before, says UCLA's Higher Education Research Institute. The American Psychological Association predicts that over 1.6 million incoming freshmen will experience a depressive episode. The National Survey of Counseling Center Directors reports that 84 percent of student counseling directors are worried about the increase in freshmen who arrive on college campuses with psychological disorders.

Kids are arriving at college already so burned out and frazzled they can hardly take advantage of the higher education they have been so thoroughly obsessed about obtaining. The hysterical ramp-up to college admissions is having a detrimental effect on health and well-being.

In response to this, counselors advise finding colleges with good mental health services. That's a fine idea, but it's not preventive. It's tantamount to trying to avert car accidents by making sure you live near a good emergency room and a competent body shop.

Parents who remain alert to the stresses their kids are under during and after the admissions process and who talk with them, empathize with them, and make sure they do activities utterly unrelated to the furtherance of their academic careers *are* acting preventively. They will give their kids a jump start on emotional wellness during the college years.

Once your kids are on campus, keep in touch. Aside from minor freak-outs over dorm-adjustment issues and papers left until the last minute, be alert to signs that they are acting unlike their usual selves. Be sure to let them know they are always welcome at home for a visit (many kids feel like "failures" if they go back home before Thanksgiving break). And bond a bit with their roommate if you can so they may feel free to contact you in the event they sense a problem.

It could be a bumpy ride, so make sure they fasten their seat belts. While you're at it, be sure to buckle up yourself.

A NEW BALL GAME

Here's another freshman year stressor to look out for: Once on campus, even a high school star will find that no one knows, or much cares, what a big fish they were in high school. The realization that one has to begin anew can be humbling, but it won't be debilitating if they feel secure not so much in what they've done but in who they are. That's where you can help. Remind them it's not about the past, and let them know the depths of your faith in them.

Secret #93
Distance Is **Relative**

Studies show that the perception that the distance from home is "just right" plays a large role in a freshman's positive adjustment to college life. But what does that mean to any individual student? One kid's "just right" may feel like light-years across the galaxy to another, and still another may experience exactly the same number of miles from home as not nearly far enough.

The comfort level is actually more about emotional distance than miles. Most freshmen want to experience a certain amount of independence, yet still feel like they're more than welcome back at the nest when they want some R & R and TLC. With this in mind, it's probably best not to rent out or renovate their rooms the moment they set one foot out the door. It's also a good idea to stay put for a while if you can, so your rookie college student has a familiar home to return to. Like lots of loving but weary parents, you may have long dreamed of moving into an adults-only gated community with a golf course once you put in your requisite eighteen years. But dreaming a bit longer won't kill you, and it will also give you time to improve your game.

Figuring out how much and how often—and just plain how—to keep in touch with your freshman is also important in shaping their perception of optimum distance. Cell phones and text messaging make it possible to stay in almost constant contact. So do spy satellites and electronic monitoring ankle bracelets, for that matter. But, as you can imagine, most kids want a little breathing room. E-mail is nice: simple, easily accessible, fairly unobtrusive. The best thing to do is ask your kid their preference and then be prepared to amend initial ideas on the subject through a little trial and error.

Should you show up for Parents' Weekend? That's an unequivocal yes. No matter what they say, or don't say, they want you there. Come bearing care packages like you did when they were at sleepaway camp. Come to think of it, care packages are always—I repeat, always—welcome. Stuff them with edibles reminiscent of home, and, magically, the miles will melt away. Over the coming years, your child may experience the dawning reality that perhaps one can't always go home again, but one can eat a homemade cookie or a bagel from the old corner deli. And somehow that makes it all feel all right.

Secret #94

Fewer Walk on the **Wild** Side

Remember when you were in college and did stupid, reckless stuff? *Yes, you.* Well, now you'll worry about whether your offspring will do the same. But this should make you feel better: Of late, a number of schools, including Princeton and the University of Michigan, have banned that cardinal sin of youthful gregariousness—streaking. In fact, Michigan students who partake in the Naked Mile midnight race must now wear underwear or face charges of indecent exposure.

And you were worried.

COLLEGE CRAZES—YESTERDAY AND TODAY

1920s—raccoon coats, the Charleston

1930s—sitting on flagpoles, swallowing goldfish

1950s—phone-booth stuffing

1960s—student strikes, be-ins, love-ins

1970s—streaking, toga parties, *Saturday Night Live*

1980s—MTV, video games

1990s—body piercing, raves

2000+—résumé building, jockeying for internships, prepping for GREs

A Mind Is a **Wonderful** Thing to Change

Every year, hordes of eager freshmen arrive at colleges and universities all over the land, presumably with the intent to stay for some reasonable length of time until they earn their bachelor's degrees. Six years later, according to the U.S. General Accounting Office, only 51 percent of them have done so. Of the remaining 49 percent, some dropped out, but the majority transferred to another institution.

Rethinking one's college selection appears to start sooner rather than later. According to the *Chronicle of Higher Education*, one-third of new college students don't return to their originally selected school in sophomore year. For a variety of reasons, they changed their minds.

Isn't that something? In high school, one's choice of college seems like a be-all-and-end-all decision. Yet, nearly half of all students make a change in plan. Rather than signifying failure, their willingness to adapt and modify their plans proves they've learned a valuable life lesson: All decisions are based on probability, not certainty.

The idea that we can predict anything with complete accuracy was scientifically dispelled by quantum mechanics. The Heisenberg uncertainty principle tells us that we cannot even predict where a particle will be from moment to moment. Yes, we can say that an atom will be at some location with a 99 percent probability, but there will be a 1 percent probability that it will be somewhere else (in fact, there will be a small but finite probability that it will be found across the universe).

The uncertainty principle is depicted by this equation:

$$dp \times dx > h / (2 \times pi) = \text{Planck's constant} / (2 \times pi).$$

But my grandmother used to describe much the same phenomenon when she greeted every pronouncement of a detailed plan with, "You never know where you're going until you get there." (It was somewhat annoying at the time, Grandma, but now I get it.)

I know you hope your kid will be among the 51 percent to pick and stick. You want them to find the perfect school and earn their degree with nary a detour, let alone a foray across the universe. Perhaps they will. But there are worse things than changes of plan. Often, in fact, the best of what life has to offer seems to arise from a serendipitous source that prompts enormous changes at the last minute.

Maybe your kid will stay at the school at which they start out. Maybe they'll go elsewhere—a smaller school, a bigger school, a school with a major in which they've become newly intrigued. Whatever they do, they're off on a great adventure. Give them a hug, a cell phone, and permission to improvise. You'll know where they're going when they get there.

Secret #96

There's Always **Grad** School

In four years' time, there's a good chance the same kid you're so worried about today will be undergoing another admissions marathon—this time aimed at getting into graduate school. Why should this make you feel better? Certainly the demographics for that scenario don't look especially encouraging. In 1969, only about one hundred thousand Americans earned graduate and professional degrees. By 2001, the number was six hundred thousand. The number of those pursuing advanced degrees continues to rise.

There are, though, some factors that make grad-school admissions a bit easier to deal with. By the time students apply to grad school, they're usually pretty clear about what it is they want to do. They know what schools offer programs that suit their very particular needs, skills, and career goals. The hype factor in school selection, while not absent (yes, grad schools are ranked by that newsweekly), is not as intense as it is at the undergrad level. What's more, since more students pay for their grad-school tuition out of their own pockets, often through teaching or research assistantships, they are more apt to seek a pragmatic return on investment and to keep their expectations realistic.

And then there's you. With your kid having actually undertaken several years of college education and, in many cases, lived away from home for some time, you might not feel so compelled to stay up nights worrying about their grad-school applications. Or you might, but you'll be too old and tired to stay up past the evening news. Or you might, but your nursing-home attendants will convince you that it would place too great a strain on your heart. Either way, chances are your input will not nearly be as critical then as you think it is now. So that's the good news. Or the bad news. Well, in any case, that's the news about grad school.

ANOTHER SHOT AT THE BRASS RING

For those who still crave a brand-name school to put on their résumé, grad school offers another shot at the top tier—even for those students who did not get into their first-choice undergrad college. At last check, only 15 percent of the first-year class at Harvard Law have been Harvard undergraduates.

Secret #97
Bragging Rights Never Expire

Once upon a time, an undergraduate named Fred Smith earned what he recalls "his usual C" on a college term paper that laid out his idea for an overnight delivery service. Years later, he used the same concept to found Federal Express.

Once upon a time, a would-be filmmaker was rejected from the prestigious film schools at both UCLA and USC. He went to California State, Long Beach, where he made several student films. Later, he made a few more, including *ET, Close Encounters of the Third Kind, Schindler's List,* and *Saving Private Ryan.*

Will your kid's ultimate potential be spotted by admissions officers or even by their professors? Maybe; maybe not. Actually, probably not.

Patience.

There is no statute of limitations on parental bragging rights.

Secret #98

They Will Come **Home** Again

Parental anxiety abhors a vacuum. Once the letters of acceptance arrive, your admissions anxiety is bound to be replaced by empty-nest anxiety. It's only natural to be apprehensive about how your child's imminent departure will affect their relationship with you. Certainly that bond will change and evolve.

But if you're worried that the start of their college years means they won't come home again, *come on.*

They will come home, and they'll bring their laundry with them. Sometimes they'll even bring their friends and their friends' laundry. As for statistics on the numbers of kids who move back home *after* college, well, never mind; you're not ready for those yet. But I will tell you this: that demographic group has become so large that it has even been given a name of its own: Twixters.

The moniker sounds like a breakfast cereal, but it's meant to connote a young adult suspended between college and real life. It's a well-known social phenomenon that once a group has a name, its ranks seem to swell even more (remember hippies and yuppies?), so don't rule out the possibility that your offspring may re-turn to the nest and may do so for a prolonged period of time.

What to do? Enjoy the intermittent respites of the next four years while you can. Don't fret too much about the postcollege years (yet), but, on the other hand, don't be too swift to get rid of that PlayStation or turn the family room into the library you've always wanted. Meanwhile, buy more fabric softener. You never know when the doorbell will ring and a bag of soiled socks, fol-lowed by a scruffy freshman, will cross your threshold.

Chapter 13: Extra **Credit**

Secret #99

Enjoy Your Life

Want to know what to do with yourself while your kid's off at college? Take pleasure in your life. The more you practice being grateful for the good things in it, the less you will feel that your kid has to compensate for any missed opportunities or failed expectations.

Don't feel guilty about letting them know that they're not having all the fun, that you're having some as well. It will give them comfort and something to look forward to. Be a poster parent for happiness.

Oh, and if there's something you regret not having done, do it.

The **Ultimate** Acceptance Letter

Dear (Daughter/Son):

We know it's been a tough time. We're glad the matter of where you're going to college is settled. We're sorry if there were times when we made ourselves a nuisance over the whole thing. As you know, being a nuisance is part of the parental job description. Okay, it's a big part. You can't say we didn't do our job.

It's going to seem strange with you gone, especially at first. It will be awfully quiet around here. And noticeably neater and cleaner. Plus, we won't have to argue so much about who gets to watch the big-screen TV. Nevertheless, we'll miss you like crazy. Mom has already started looking for those kindergarten drawings to rehang on the fridge. And did you know we've still got about six sets of your clay handprints? Remember that time . . . oh, never mind. (We promised ourselves we wouldn't go there.)

We just want to say we hope you know you're always welcome back home. You don't have to wait until Thanksgiving. Just show up. Or we'll come get you. Or we'll send you a ticket. Meanwhile, don't forget to call.

We got that new family plan with unlimited minutes, remember? And then there's e-mail. And what's a good time to instant-message? (Oops, we promised ourselves we wouldn't go there, either.)

These four years will go fast, but at the end of them you'll be, well, if not a new person then an expanded one (hey, and not just because the dining-hall food isn't as healthy as Mom's cooking, ha-ha). We're eager to watch you become more of your future self, to continue to witness you becoming your complete self.

We wish you a wonderful college experience. We wish you friends that you will keep for a lifetime. We wish you at least one professor who will change the way you look at the world forevermore. We wish you the courage to take on a challenge, even if it means risking failure—because that's not failure at all. Most of all, we wish you the ability to sleep through really loud music and stay awake through really dull lectures.

Okay, we're trying not to get maudlin here. In any case, it all adds up to one thing: We love you. We don't mean to embarrass you, but every once in a while we just have to say it. We know you love us, too, because if you didn't, you wouldn't have read this far. So, when you speak of us at college—and you will—be kind. We did our best—and you are our best.

Love,
Your parents

Secret #101

Crib Sheet

The Ten Commandments of Applying

(as Applied to You and Your Kid)

1. Be realistic.
2. Don't fall for hype.
3. Don't follow the crowd.
4. Maintain a positive attitude.
5. Don't neglect the details.
6. Don't be paralyzed by test results.
7. Don't take rejection personally.
8. Take a long view of life.
9. Trust in serendipity.
10. Be happy for each other—you've all made it this far.

A F T E R W O R D

Realizing that many of you who have a child applying to college now will have other children applying down the road, I'd like to take out my crystal ball for a moment and speculate about the future. Will things be any calmer in years to come? In a word: yes.

Things will begin to change after the year 2010. The Echo Boomer generation, the proverbial pig in a python currently swelling the system, will have peaked, and the great high school senior bubble will begin to diminish slightly. The number of kids graduating high school will taper off, and with it the current extraordinarily huge demand for freshman college slots.

College admissions comprise a market—and all markets are cyclical. When demand drops, supply rises. Many institutions of higher learning will find that they have put into place prices and standards that cannot be sustained in a more relaxed market. Both will have to be adjusted.

The cost of a college education, while unlikely to plummet, may begin to level off at many schools, at least beginning to correspond more realistically with the rate of inflation. In addition, educational consumers, out of increased necessity and increased savvy, are likely to develop more creative strategies for economic coping. These will include:

* *More kids taking time off in-between high school and college.* By working for a year or two, high school graduates will save money to

fund part of their education. This decision will not be stigmatized. Indeed, it will be increasingly recognized that work experience can help kids consider what it is they really want to study and what skills they really want to develop.

* *More students starting their college careers at community colleges.* More enrollees will enter community college with the specific goal of getting an inexpensive but very viable start to a college education and transferring after two years. Admissions in this market may become more selective, and prices may rise to some degree. Nevertheless, these institutions will honor their mission to serve the community as best as resources allow.

* *More work-study options.* There will be more colleges modeled after the College of the Ozarks, where students earn their entire tuition through working at college-sponsored endeavors. Other schools will modify the model, and more partial tuition coverage will be the result.

* *More "vocational" college options.* There will be more colleges modeled after the Wentworth Institute of Technology in Boston, which offers a bachelor's degree in construction management that prepares graduates to manage large projects or to run smaller home-building-related businesses. Dozens of schools are already offering similar programs, and their numbers will grow exponentially as a matter of economic pragmatism. Such colleges will, like Wentworth, offer a combination of lectures, labs, and paid internships.

Still polishing my crystal ball, I see a few more things on the horizon. You don't want to know about the Red Sox. Ah, but this one has to do with standardized testing. Although large universities will continue to rely on the SATs as a way of controlling the cost of processing admissions, smaller schools will probably position themselves to attract a growing number of students who will "just say no" to the SAT and its attendant stress. Although these smaller schools (like Bates College) will look at SATs if submitted, they will not require them.

Now for a bit of irritating news. (Yes, it's always something.) College marketing in general will become more and more aggressive. By the start of the next decade, you won't be able to tune into a television show or click on an Internet search engine without seeing an ad for an institution of higher learning. Your younger children will likely be deluged with mailing pieces before they're out of braces. Be strong. Recycle the paper. Everything you learned in the preceding pages about doing your own diligent research will still apply when it comes to finding the right school for the right student.

The best news of all is that although many things will change, one thing will remain the same: Parents are going to remain committed to getting their children the best education possible. That's always been a primary goal of American families, as well it ought to be. Remain focused, remain calm. It will all turn out okay!

About the Author

ARLENE MATTHEWS is the founder of Your College Coach (www.yourcollegecoach.com), an admissions advising service. She is the author of seven books on parenting and self-help topics, including *The Seven Keys to Calm.* Her work has appeared in such publications as *Money* magazine, the *San Francisco Chronicle*, the *Washington Examiner*, and *Poets & Writers*. Her books have been translated into five languages.

A college psychology instructor, Arlene also runs stress management and college application seminars for parents' groups and corporations. She lives in Fair Haven, New Jersey, with her husband and teenage son. She welcomes your thoughts and questions on the college admissions experience and may be reached at arlene@yourcollegecoach.com.